APOSTLE MOSLEY

RANDOM THOUGHTS OF GOD

Extraordinary Ideas for Ordinary Folks

Bishop W. Ralph Mangum

ISBN: 978-1-60383-318-9

Published by:
Holy Fire Publishing
717 Old Trolley Road
Attn: Suite 6, Publishing Unit #116
Summerville, SC 29485

www.ChristianPublish.com

Cover Designer: Jay Cookingham

Printed in the United States of America and the United Kingdom

ACKNOWLEDGMENT

I am eternally grateful to the following people for their support in writing this book:

My loving and very supportive wife, Dr. Shirley B. Mangum, who endured the many nights alone while I toiled to get this manuscript finished.

Deacon Thomas and Sister Nise Hampleton for their untiring devotion to The Total Man Ministries, Inc., and to me, their pastor, and the Lord Jesus Christ.

Minister Noah and Sister Ayona Boston who have always been very supportive of The Total Man Ministries, Inc., and their pastor.

Brother-in-law, Mr. Charles Beckwith, for his contribution to the completion of this manuscript.

Sister-in-law, Mrs. Eleanore Jones, for her prayerful and emotional support when things were not very promising. She always had words of encouragement.

Sister Annette Boatwright.

To my Lord and Savior Jesus Christ who is ever present in my life and has blessed me beyond all my reasonable and unreasonable expectations.

Foreword

Throughout history, we humans have been drawn inexorably to wise maxims or aphorisms. We often refer to the sayings of great individuals such as Confucius, King Solomon, and Jesus. Our attachment to such things is also underlined by the hundreds of sayings propagated by our forefathers. Without our even trying, many pop into our minds: "Don't cry over spilt milk," "A rolling stone gathers no moss," "Waste not, want not," and on they go...

What is it about these brief, pithy statements that grab our attention? First, we typically tend to appreciate simplicity and most are simple and straightforward. Second, usually they express an insight or bit of wisdom, some better way humans can behave or live. Third, they're easy to remember and quote. Fourth, many people have significantly improved the quality of their lives by observing these concepts.

W. Ralph Mangum has obviously thought long and hard about the sayings in this book. Many may be derived from personal experience through the decades, whether positive or negative. I can honestly say that you will benefit from the study of many of the truths of this volume. You may not agree with every single one, but now and then you will likely smile and shake your head as a quotation zings home to your mind and heart. And you will purpose to be a better person or a better Christian based on insights and instructions set forth here.

Reverend Mangum covers many relevant topics and I have tried to organize them clearly by subject for your convenience. Don't feel as if you must complete the book in one sitting. In fact, the book is probably better appreciated and digested in small doses. So have it handy somewhere in the house and just pick it up when you have a few minutes or need some extra inspiration. Enjoy!

-Dr. Steve Fortosis

Table of Contents

How Wisdom can be Your most Valuable Possession

Why walk in darkness and face needless dangers, when walking in the light will show the way?

A soft glove may hide a clenched fist and a kiss in the dark may hide a disdainful look.

The words "I love you," has brought many to an untimely end.

Supposed wisdom can come from a fool, but the wise will know the difference and abide in safety.

When listening to good advice, be careful you don't fall asleep and miss a cue.

The disclaimer "Reasonable facsimile thereof" is suggesting that you will accept something less than what you paid for.

Wisdom does not come from academic study or philosophical curiosity but evolves and grows within the spirit of a committed person.

Wisdom is not a product of academic achievement but spiritual connectivity with the Author of all wisdom as manifested in humility.

Wasted effort is not in vain if the goal was worthwhile and the end results in a blessing.

The wise look before they leap but the unwise leap before they look.

Someone said, "Know your friends and your enemies can't hurt you," but I say, "Know thyself and the enemy can't come in to you."

Reason is in the hands of the wise, but a fool is fast to speak and slow to understand.

Wisdom is not the tool of a show-off, talking head, or academic nerd, but a gift bestowed on those who can live the life of the Giver of wisdom.

A bird in the hand is not better than two in the bush if I own the bush.

To know wisdom the seeker must seek the source of all wisdom and that alone will suffice the desire to know. The narcissistic desire to be known is not wisdom but carnality, for carnality is closer to the basest of men.

Knowing the rules of the road do not make one a good driver just as knowing a truth does not make one wise. It is the one who applies the truth that is wise.

Some say that raw knowledge is golden and to whatever degree this may be, wisdom will trump it every time, for she cannot be defeated. Contested, devalued, many will decry, but wisdom is never defeated, for her author and giver is Almighty God.

One of the secrets to long life is right preparation, for bad preparation can hasten an early death.

Excitement based on quick observation can dull the hard-fought wisdom of experience.

The brain is capable of ever-increasing wisdom as determined by the mind's willingness to explore and retain the things of God.

Think through matters while anticipating outcomes and avoid needless journeys into areas of confusion, anger, frustration and disappointment.

Who is the smarter, he who follows by instinct or he who is led?

Who is the wiser, the sage for his wisdom or the prophet for a relationship with God?

The ways of God mean gain and wise is the person who walks in them.

Every angel of light is not sent from God, but the wisdom of God will save the pure in heart.

A wise individual professes not wisdom but humility under the awesome power of the hand of Almighty God. All else counts as nothing, for we are nothing more than sinners saved by grace.

Understanding is free to all who will partake of her, but ignorance can extract a heavy penalty.

Desperation can ignite a desperate person to accomplish miraculous things under fire, but wisdom can save a house from catching fire.

Don't burn the house you last slept in because it may rain tomorrow. Retracing a path to defeat can weary the mind.

The wise look before they leap. The fool's only concern is the gathering crowd of spectators.

The need for godly wisdom is ever present in every man and woman. But the realization of that need is diminished in the heart of a fool.

True wisdom is not the wisdom of mankind at all, but the wisdom of God handed down to us to accomplish the will of God on earth.

Running in light is safer than walking in darkness because light is the sustainer of the godly. Even a walk in the dark is unprofitable for the wise.

Knowledge is the goal of the ungodly but, understanding, the mainstay of the righteous.

Commitment is the heart of stability, and peace is the fruit of a made-up mind.

"A word to the wise" is not always wisdom and should be received with contemplation.

Never leave your heart unattended while your emotions are on a roller coaster.

A person knows a thing but lives what she believes, and this is not necessarily best.

Hear the whole of a matter and avoid the appearance of a fool.

If one person's reasoning is another's folly, which person is to be followed?

Who is more deserving of respect? The one who knows how to move a thing and does nothing or the one who does not know and attempts to move the thing?

He who knows how to achieve yet refuses to accomplish a thing is worse than one he who professes to know and knows not. For the one who boasts of his understanding has proved his lack of wisdom by his lack of activity. The other is only ignorant.

Good advice in the ear of the wise is marrow to the bones but fodder in the ear of a fool.

If you must accommodate your enemy, cuddle him close and watch his hands. And beware of meetings at midnight or lonely walks along the pier.

Beware of the friends of your enemy lest they grab you with a handshake and snare you with a smile.

Know your enemy and face him, but beware of his friend in your rear, for he is unseen.

Who can know the end of a thing except he knows the beginning? And is the beginning of a thing better than the end?

A godly individual only benefits from that to which she is capable of reacting wisely.

A wise adventurer will not enter into a thing with an obscured exit, for who knows how far he can advance?

Never arouse a sleeping enemy; just know where he is.

If you know the heart of your enemy, you can steal his plan and take away his stealth.

A house with many shared keys may be your home today and your prison tomorrow and who will know you're gone?

A jar half full is better than no jar at all and with wise use can last just as long if used with discipline.

Knowledge is golden and can accomplish many things otherwise impossible, but wisdom is the crown of all and can save the day.

Who is the greater of two? The one who gives his life to save another or the one who devotes his life to teaching others to live? Who is the greater, the one who teaches another to fish or the one who provides the fish?

Bitter and sweet water cannot come from the same source at the same time, but one can change his or her preference for one or the other.

Darkness in one's life will always continue until the understanding is opened by the dawning of a new day.

The longer a person lives the more he knows, though his eyes grow dim with age. But is it always best to live longer?

Not knowing the whole of a matter can allow folks to lose their way.

To know something and do nothing may be considered prudent, but to activate what one knows can be great gain.

Great knowledge without use is not beneficial and will eventually die for lack of use.

A wise person will not be caught in a web of deceit of them who pretend righteousness.

God protects those of His who are wise and humble in spirit and their feet shall not slip or their grasp lose its hold.

Who knows the way of destruction better than the one destroyed who has returned to describe it?

There are secrets that no one can or will know so why do we yet strive to gain unlawful entry to places we know nothing of?

Discern the times and the seasons and wisdom will direct your path to understanding.

A blind man cannot see the error of his ways and is in need of someone else to guide him. Not knowing a truth does not make one obsolete, just needy.

Is it wiser to stay and resolve an issue than to retreat and possibly fight again? They who make a hasty retreat might have to face their enemy again.

Can humans understand that which they have heard except they first be taught?

A human mind cannot function wisely unless it has a viable host.

Learning How to Think

Better the simple mind of a child than the mind of a genius that stumbles over simple truth.

The light of God is ever present to illuminate one's path into eternity.

Someone once said; "The mind is a terrible thing to waste" and that is true if the products of the mind are fruitless.

Knowing oneself is a lifetime endeavor, and every day a new challenge.

The mind is a world of unsearchable depth, and its limits known only by One.

A human is driven or led by the will but the heart must approve.

The soul, free of the mind of Christ is a in a perpetual free-fall and its rapid descent must end in destruction. It is like a child with a machine gun; everything around him is in danger, for his parameters are boundless and everyone around him is fair game.

Peace of mind, spiritual stability, world view, immediate and future goals are much dependent upon one's view of self.

In the mind of a child there is mischief, in the mind of a woman perhaps is cunning , but in the mind of a man, struggle, and, of that, no end. But for one born in Christ there is hope.

A mind without purpose, a will without a goal, a soul without God equals walking destruction.

Right thinking is a matter of perception; positive thinking, a matter of selective choosing. In summary, "The steps of a good man are ordered by the Lord."

If thy rattled mind shall rule thy soul, thy future shall be in doubt.

Does common sense apply to the uncommon man?

Miniscule thinking by a miniscule mind produces miniscule results and such efforts soon die.

The mind is an awful thing to waste and the self-abused body is the consequence of an uncontrolled mind.

How can a man receive or understand that which he has not seen except that which is unseen give him the desire and ability to receive?

Affairs of the heart are often just that, because the mind knows better.

The mind and the heart can be a "Dr. Jekyll and Mr. Hide" in the affairs of men in the absence of a Chris- centered life.

Uncontrolled fear results in panic and paranoia and discipline is far removed.

Some critical thinkers question the need and reality of a thing and some don't think at all.

It is suggested to "know your enemy" which implies that one will have an advantage if he knows the abilities of his enemy. For how can a man defeat that which he cannot see or understand?

Knowing one's limits will help a man manage his resources well and avoid needless frustration on the part of himself and others. And it may provide a new beginning for another.

If we be in Christ to the glory of God, all of what humans know is only the beginning of what we are capable of knowing as we transcend our mortal habitation for immortality.

Everything a Christian thinks is preparation for the occasion when he will be immortalized. And all things will be revealed in him when he becomes one in the mind of Christ and the two are One.

It's not only what humans see in this life to beware of but the things unseen, for they can come upon us unawares.

In an attempt to break free of a critical situation, try not to say or do things in an act of desperation. Do not make the situation worse. Think!

Never be rash in arriving at a conclusion until you hear the whole of the matter.

Rash decisions often bring quick execution in the name of rationality.

Most people do whatever their mind suggests based on their emotions. It is often wrong to follow one's first inclination.

Is a human more responsible for what he contemplates before he acts or more responsible for what he does before contemplation?

How to Avoid Pride and Conceit

He who beats his own drum will not have time to hear yours.

The self-righteous have no need of a higher spiritual authority for they are a god unto themselves.

When popularity and pride are kindred spirits, peace is far off.

The atheists say there is no God, and the super-pious think they hold God in their hip pocket. Who is the fool?

Pride comes before a fall and is a precursor for destruction.

The quest for acclamation can cause one to lose focus on a distant priority and settle for immediate gratification to much sorrow when the light of day comes.

Rivers of living waters cannot flow from a cistern filled with the pride of life, for everything produces after its kind.

A person's ego can drive a hard bargain and his stealth command the night.

Mortal men are vast in number but few know the wisdom of almighty God and, of the prideful ignorant, there is no end.

If you believe you're the "Cat's meow" you're a fool about to fall, for there is a dog lurking in the wings.

The path to greatness is littered with dreams of grandeur.

The mind of mortal humanity is a gift from God, but when mankind does not observe and obey the laws of Almighty God he will find that there are parameters, not to limit his will to explore, but to control his tendency to seek things he is not prepared to face and to curb his intolerable pride.

Physical beauty can be a gift from God used to glorify Him or the object of the foolish: a self-imposed image used to glorify self.

Those who toot their own horn have not a respectable horn to toot.

If people look pretty only on the outside, they will ultimately look ugly indeed.

They who gloat at themselves in the mirror are blinded by their deceit and are truly "full" of themselves.

Deceit has many forms of captivation: deceit in looks, deceit in thinking, deceit in actions, and deceit of self. A deceptive person cannot be trusted for his allegiance is to no one in particular and is for sale to the highest bidder.

A cold heart has no bounds, for it is incapable of fair play and rationale is a topic for the weak.

No mortal man can intelligently present him- or herself as a living god, for he or she is not capable of creating and maintaining him- or herself independent of all else in the universe and is forever subject to universal death.

Destruction is in the heart of an arrogant man for he is not fearful of slandering celestial beings which he knows nothing of and respects even less.

God does not always stop the perpetuation of evil nor does He control an ego-centric mind, but the wages of sin is death and "Vengeance is mine," says the Lord, "and I will repay."

If a person knows evil's fruits and does what is not right in the sight of Almighty God, why does he still do evil unless he is a conceited fool?

Mark the man who imagines that he can avoid death by his own power. Even he must go to the pit, for none shall escape. Enoch escaped death, but he worshipped God and was translated.

Times are changing faster than most people can conceive, and yet the vast number of people on the face of the earth refuses to acknowledge the existence and presence of a holy, righteous God who is ultimately in control of the events that surround us. We are yet leaning to our own understanding.

How can an individual consistently enjoy, even revel, in the goodness of the earth and not consider the bad and his eventual end?

Humans love to be sensationalized because sensationalizing caters to the senses by arousing certain feelings that oftentimes demand immediate gratification. These are sometimes sought in harmful ways.

A person's view of himself is often distorted because his pride blocks his view.

Many profess knowledge of things they know nothing about and curse things celestial to their own damnation. Those who follow them will suffer their own humiliation.

Can a person declare her own wisdom and be wise still? For if she be wise, then why must she declare her wisdom except to win those in doubt?

A selfish person cannot believe he has done wrong because he must continually justify himself.

We cannot successfully serve two Gods for long. We will serve one and hate other or serve neither and hate both.

Manipulation is a choice made by humans to seek to force what they desire.

A spirit of self importance is in direct opposition to the presence of God in one's life, for God is holy and there is none more relevant to human beings than He.

In the celebration of our achievements in various fields of endeavor we have become drunk on self- adulation to the extent that we acknowledge no one other than us personally, and there is none greater than we. We totally exclude everyone and everything else. Whether one agrees with this observation is not important because the total narcissism that is spreading nationally and even globally will surely come to pass and is not dependent upon any person's acceptance.

Joy is the Spiritual Perfection of Happiness

Know the source of your joy and you'll know whom you can trust.

Happiness is dependent upon the circumstances in your life, but joy is a safer and, therefore, a more crucial ingredient.

Don't share your joy with a fool lest he set your dream on fire.

If I can give you happiness, I can also take it away. Your happiness should not be dependent upon the happenings in your life. Joy is a better and safer ingredient.

Happiness will always be supplanted by joy because joy requires no external or carnal manifestation but is the fruit of righteousness shown in holiness.

The pursuit of happiness is an ongoing endeavor and is never satisfied for she is totally dependent on the right circumstances which are never found. Consequently, emotional attachments never provide happiness but only for a season.

Don't lose your way in the glitter of superficiality and pass a road to joy less obvious, for the happiness of the moment has blinded many.

The giver of your happiness can also be the captain of your ship.

Don't lose your way in the glitter of superficiality, for the happiness of the moment has blinded many. You may pass the narrow path to joy unawares.

Joy is a spiritual byproduct of adopting, believing, witnessing the laws of Almighty God.

Happiness can be defined as waiting for the *"practitioners of luck"* to throw a bone your way.

Never allow a thief to reside in your midst for he will steal your goods and the enemy will steal your joy.

The dawning of a new day brings light and promises of deliverance from the darkness of night.

Laughter is good for the soul and the injured spirit within, but a frown kills them both.

Joy can be the source of everlasting peace and thy soul will not suffer for lack of rest.

Is temporary happiness better than no happiness at all? Is long life a key to happiness or happiness a key to long life? Is temporary happiness a precursor to future pain?

A man's face may radiate many images but few are smiles from the heart.

The morning brings renewed spirits, new activities and refreshed spirits. Why not for you?

As precious as the spirit of Happiness is, it is transitory at best because it is dependent upon circumstances or "happenings" in one's life as opposed to joy which comes from the peace that passes all understanding because it comes from the Lord Jesus Christ.

Joy is the key to everlasting peace and the tranquil soul will not suffer from lack of sleep.

When two sons or daughters of creation rise up together, early in the morning to celebrate the dawning of a new day, God is glorified.

There is no greater joy found among in the world than knowing the peace and presence of Almighty God in one's life.

Can a person know his beginning and contemplate his end, yet still avoid a sense of doom?

Why does a human pine for the past and obsess with the future instead of enjoying the present?

Why Laziness Leaves you Desolate

Everything produces after its own kind, so doing nothing produces nothing.

"Watch your friends and your enemies can't hurt you," someone suggested. Well, I watched his house all night and he never came out.

Laziness is a form of slow death. The urge to "get moving" is an inward warning that death is approaching.

The human body was created to require constant revitalizing without which each member begins a slow decline in strength and bulk.

There are many kinds of addictions and one of the most grievous is the addiction of laziness, for the fruit of laziness is more laziness and more frequent need.

Those who constantly and needlessly give to the lazy will be responsible for the birth of another addict in the world.

Learning is an invitation to greatness but a lazy man will die in his easy chair awaiting a free hand.

Abundant walks through the park, too many stops to rest, and a lackadaisical attitude can hasten a trip into eternity.

A man's future is judged by his work ethic.

An unguarded moment during a period of leisure may open gates to destruction, for a sleeping individual is easy prey.

Waiting forever for a helping hand can stagnate the will, and help will be in vain.

The ways of a lazy person are fraught with despair, danger, and ever increasing problems and the future is surely in doubt.

The simplest things in life are often the most attainable, but cheap food does not always provide the proper nutritional support for mind and body.

Cheap prices often produce cheap results for cheap people.

The poor, unwise man seeks out the worthless and is forever poor. And the beat goes on.

Is wasted time in the affairs of humanity a violation of the stewardship duties bestowed upon us by Almighty God?

Man was created to work long hours or his body would begin to fall apart and the labor of hard work was for the original sin. So laziness is not godly but an affront to the will of almighty God.

When humans are not productive they are squandering the abilities God has instilled in them and when we do not use a God-given gift we lose it.

What is Genuine Love and why is it Indispensable?

True love can never be bartered.

Genuine love can be the catalyst for all things good, but words spoken in anger can defeat a nation.

A hug can enhance the promise of a good day, but a kiss can seal the deal.

One of the secrets to long life is right preparation but bad preparation can hasten an early death.

Words of love and words of endearment are members of the same family and should generate deeds in action without which a wise man will not follow.

True love is prolonged but a season of lust is soon revealed for what it is.

There are those who profess to love God and those who profess not to love God and both can demonstrate that fact, but the life of one is void of any lasting good.

I show you a paradox: Among those things common to mankind is breaking bread together but so is withholding food from a hungry child.

Love resides in the heart, is manifested in the hands, extolled by the mouth, and glorifies God.

True love is an emotion whose potential is available to all who desire it---an emotion not many are willing to exhibit. Many desire its benefits, and few are willing to pay the price.

The love of God sets an individual free of his natural inclination to love self rather than God.

One can be alone and not lonely and every house is not a home, and every lover is not a friend, but a means to an end.

Looking for love in the wrong places will soon reveal the futility of the search and the ease in which one can be fooled.

Loving God makes us truly alive, and accepting the love of God for us should be our ultimate desire, but many are oblivious to both.

Feed your enemies with a long handled spoon and put not your hand in his mouth less he bite you in your haste.

In today's secular, humanistic society the expression "I love you" has in many minds evolved into nothing more than a plea for immediate acceptance and recognition by the hearer for the speaker.

True love is forgiving, sharing, non-judgmental, and compassionate. Last but not least, it is protective and knows no bounds.

The love of God will saturate the mind of His saints with the mind of Christ, and fill the heart of His Saints with the love of Christ manifested in jars of clay, and the mouth will speak the words of Christ.

War and peace are opposing spirits but love will abide.

The beauty of love is that it is encompassing and non-judgmental; the danger of love is that it is easily feigned.

One shows love by her action in a matter and another shows love by her lack of action in a matter. Are not both acting wisely?

Love has an opposing force that we know as carnal which strives to be equal or greater than love. Carnality embraces all that is of a fleshly nature, and is employed by Satan to trick the family of God into believing that carnality is a demonstration of love of one human for another based on feelings and emotions. But the love of God (Agape) manifested in Jesus Christ is far superior to our emotions and can overcome every carnal emotion and observation, for it is the perfect antidote for everything ungodly.

A plea for help is not always verbally expressed and a plea for help and a plea for understanding are two different things.

A plea for help can be interpreted as "I need help in getting out of this mess!" A plea for understanding can best be interpreted as "I don't necessarily want your intervention, but your compassion."

A judgmental mentality knows not a spirit of compassion and understanding is far off.

Can a human conceive the love of God if the Spirit of God is not in him?

The love of God constrains one to do what is right and to be responsible for her actions and attitudes.

It has been proven that we cannot love two Gods for we will hold fast to one and hate the other. And sooner or later we will have to make a choice as to which one we will follow.

Can a human love another more than himself without the power of God in his life?

Is the term "selfish" a necessary act of self preservation or an attitude of possessiveness?

Which is more desirable in a relationship, knowing one is loved by declaration or knowing one is loved by what one sees?

Everything produces after its own kind, beginning with the Creator of all things who is Love incarnate and who can manifest this love in human beings. Humanity has the ability to love but the freedom
to pick and choose who and what to love has caused us to often destroy that will in others and the consequences are often devastating.

Love begins with God and is passed down in a transcending order to humans, who must first love God and with that, comes the will and ability to love ourselves and then others. And when that "chain of love" is broken, the opposite replaces or fills the vacuum created by the absence of love.

The things that a human cherishes most can be the things that offer the greatest potential for harm.

It is said that the more energy individuals give of themselves the less energy they have for themselves. If this is done unwillingly frustration is the result. It must be propelled by the love of God.

Pure love returned or acknowledged will perpetuate more of the same, for God is love personified.

There is a sort of self-righteous, covert glee when some Christians tell hostile pagans that their destiny is hell. Every human being who chooses to be lost rather than serve the living God should break our hearts. The Bible declares, "Hell is enlarged daily."

Late sleepers miss the choicest part of the day, for the first fruits are available before the hordes arrive.
The love of God rests on all His creation but, to some, the love for God seems as scarce as money for the poor. However,

those who wait upon the Lord will not live in vain and God will fight their battles.

A discerning spirit will save the man or woman of God and the love for God will propel them to destinations beyond their fondest dreams.

Why Fools come to a Bitter End

A fool for a friend is like walking a high wire; you never know when you'll fall.

A fool is known by his passions but the wise can save the day.

A self-justified lie is often revealed because the liar is known by the company he keeps.

The heart of a fool is revealed by his vast promises and the few fulfillments of them.

"Word to the wise" should never be more than just that and in the ear of the hearer find welcome retreat. But words in the ears of a fool is fodder for anger and wisdom is far removed.

"Beauty and the Beast" enjoyed monumental success and wide acclaim on Broadway in a bygone era and the title suggests two opposing entities. However reality often reveals a horrible truth: frequently the two are twin residents of the same temple.

Living without boundaries soon becomes an invitation for abuse and fools rush in where wise men never tread.

Some wallow in their shame, defend their guilt, and harbor their grudges by craving the source of each just as a dog returns to his vomit.

Lovers of lust are individuals whose range of interest casts a wide net, for their prey is plentiful in number.

Never doubt the stealth of a fool. His sting can be as deadly as an adder and darkness is his cloak and shield.

The darkness in a man is not complete ignorance, but reflects the absence of the knowledge of God, who is manifested as light.

It is hard to overcome powers not seen, to outdistance that which does not compete, or to know that which you did not create. Yet a foolish man will endeavor to excel in things not understood by mortal men and his destruction is eminent.

He who hears the whole of a matter is wise but a fool responds with premature actions.

The more a person knows, the greater the threat to himself and others, and only the discipline of a Supernatural power greater than he, can control his progress. But the fool's ultimate descent to destruction is assured, and he will be known as he is.

One must be taught to see beyond himself, and she must believe she can see. Early destruction is sure to be found in the presence of the foolish.

A wise man seeks to prolong life and promote the good in the world to the glory of God, but a fool is known for his carnal pursuits and much speaking in defense of the works of darkness. His quiver is never full and his appetite is insatiable for things of the flesh.

A fool does not always sleep, but whether he be the hunted or the hunter, he will lose.

Don't ignore flags of warning at cliff's edge. Many have lived to regret a jump into hell and their heirs are here to stay.

A man not accountable to someone will be accountable for failure.

Let not the fool say "I am wise," for his mouth will reveal the depth of his wisdom and all will know his name.

Good advice in the ear of a wise man is marrow to the bones but fodder in the ears of a fool.

Who can inflict the most harm, the one who teaches what he doesn't know or the one who believes him?

Understanding a thing is not a gamble, but gambling without understanding a thing will wreak havoc.

Why broadcast your battle plans to your enemy: for the sake of impressing him with your intelligence?

The best laid plans of men often fail for lack of wise counsel.

One concealed in the dark is prey for others who also lurk in dark places, and neither is alone.

An individual with an indifferent spirit is not a reliable ally, for he is not committed to any, not even himself.

The contemplations of a fool are a precursor to problems.

Only a fool would dare curse and slander celestial beings and tempt the Spirit of the Living God. Where is the wisdom in that, and to what end?

Where is the wisdom in challenging that which one knows not and understands even less? What does this person hope to gain? He is blinded by his own lack of understanding and his destruction is certain to come at a time he knows not.

Money offers many advantages to those who possess it, but money and a fool shall soon part company.

The one who lives by his wits will soon be outwitted and many will be amazed at his gullibility.

A great change is even at the door and the wisdom of mankind is not wisdom at all, for their knowledge is veiled in darkness.

Few know the signs and wonders to behold, but humans are fools for folly and rich in empty information. The foolish sleep on and the end is not far off.

Who knows and who among us can see that which is not readily seen by the foolish and unwise?

Volunteers for a thing often generate attitudes of jealousy in the hearts of those who do nothing.

The tendency of humans is to worship themselves or obey, worship, or believe in a great deity who demands little. In either case, mankind is a failure and less than the manifestation of God's ideal for humanity.

Why will a human labor all her life and refuse to see the futility of repeated mistakes in her labor?

Is a foolish individual born to self-destruct or does he mis-manage his affairs to the extent that self destruction is inevitable?

Self-destruction seems to be the demonstration of a foregone conclusion that things are better in another place yet unknown. The key is whether an individual is searching for God's heaven, or some non-existent fool's paradise.

Developing Relationships and Good Solid Friendships

Do sharing intimate secrets produce a friendship of trust?

True friendship is born in the heart, and a lying tongue it will not entertain.

In relationships of the heart, one cannot truly become intimate before becoming an acquaintance any more than one can drive before learning the controls of an automobile.

The depth and strength of any relationship can be determined by the persistency of invested time, shared joys and failures of those involved. In such relationships, fragmentation is not an option, for every breach demands immediate attention and personal sacrifices are maximized for the sake of the group.

Relationships based on shallow attractions almost never survive beyond the initial introductory stage because there is no solid foundation based on respect, unselfishness, shared interests and common goals. Anything less eventually becomes a chore and, what is not respected, becomes disdained.

One can be contaminated by associations. Be ever careful where you sleep or walk in the dark of night.

A closely guarded secret is no safer than the friendship of the bearer.

Respect begins with self and spreads abroad.

Advice from a friend will seek the good for thee and not exploit thy need of the moment for carnal gain.

To agree not to agree may be to postpone the inevitable.

Sometimes the best kept secret is the very one you need to share.

The higher a human climbs, the further from the bottom and the greater the hurt if he falls, so remember the same people you passed on the climb up may be the first ones encountered as you descend.

Hold on to that which is productive; discard that which is useless and encourage that which is promising but never sail on a sinking ship.

Sharing a load with a friend is good, but carrying a load for a friend is better.

If words of praise can brighten the day, broken promises cause dark thoughts.

A lying friend can cost a life and an angry witness can shield the truth.

Everyone cannot build a house or an automobile, but not everyone can help.

A man's friends are best defined by their personal sacrifices on his behalf.

The enemies of a wise man are many and his friends know him best, for his friendship is sweet and more valuable than gold.

A man's friends are best defined by their personal sacrifices on his behalf.

Business, family, and friends should never share the same dream, for no one will ever sleep.
How can two dissimilar people walk together except one is changed?

Pulling one out of a ditch may not help others, for the one rescued may be a loner.

Maintain utmost respect for your friends. Let not familiarity breed contempt.

Never put all your eggs in one basket, for your friend and business partner today may be your enemy tomorrow and your basket a fading memory.

It's never too late to say 'I'm sorry", but why wait until departure time to repent, for your time may be earlier than you think and catch you unawares.

Frequently two people meet and right away they "feel" they're in love, soul mates, meant for each other, etc. But in fact they were nothing more than two people passing in the night going in separate directions. God never meant for them to meet and establish a relationship because they were not designed for each other and consequently the relationship is fraught with everything hurtful and even dangerous from time to time. And they try and try to make it work but it is an exercise in futility. Fools do rush in where wise men never go.

A sad countenance may not imply pessimism. It might reflect the presence of true inner conflicts. Care about the inner lives of others.

Why you Must Control your Words

Words can sooth bruised feelings, repair a damaged ego, and promote great joy, but actions speak louder than words.

Don't believe everything you hear or you may regret some of your replies.

Do not tell your secrets to a fool or they may be on the morning news.

A tale bearer is acquainted with many and is a friend to none.

Evading an issue only prolongs the inevitable and the end is worse than the first.

Promises without deeds are just that, and the heart of the one who promises is soon exposed.

A secret told in secret is no longer a secret for the wall has ears and little birds are friends to all.

If the best things in life are free, why are so many people living their lives in chains?

Seven words from the heart are better than twenty words from a script.

Gentle words can either calm an aroused mind or cause a guard to fall asleep.

A man's words may reveal the contents of a troubled heart, but a desperate heart knows no bounds. Let the hearer beware.

Feeding the mind with unfruitfulness fills the heart with dead works and what comes from the mouth reveals it all.

The eye sees, the mind contemplates and the heart stores for present or future use, and the mouth speaks what the heart has stored.

He who guards his mouth is wise for it is best to be thought a fool than to speak and remove all doubt.

Words of love spoken into an injured spirit can produce peace but hateful words can kill the soul.

Words of concern spoken to a server may save your life and prolong a joyful meal.

In a dispute, the truth of a matter will most likely be found halfway between the two opposing views.

Truth sometimes appears to have an equally strong opposing view.

Needless words only prolong an argument and heighten emotional fervor.

Talk is cheap and promises are easy, but they can dethrone a king and bring his kingdom down.

Those who kiss and tell cannot hide a secret for long, for the need of recognition is too strong.

Tell what you know for sure. Truth often hangs in the balance and, without it, the guilty go free.

There are sometimes no guarantees in the promises of an individual for she too is held by the promise of another. And life goes on.

Who is the more believable: he who speaks with his mouth or he who communicates with his hands?

Don't speak evil of another, for you have much in common. In fact, only God knows the difference.

Eloquent speaking and many words are not always tools of a wise man.

A hasty mouth and fast feet invariably lead to ruinous circumstances.

Be careful what you declare, for whatever one declares is what will be his reward.

When we discover that people are not as sold out to the Lord as we are and allow that to turn to criticism, we are blocking our own path to God, for God never gives us discernment in order for us to be critical of someone else but for us to intercede.

Speaking one's mind sounds cavalier but can alienate a potential friend for life or kill a blessing on the wing.

In the land of the living there is more to be concerned about than talking to the dead.

The life and profession of an ordained man of God is full of life's contradictions, for the vast majority of earth's values and systems are in opposition to the Word of God and he as a worker in Christ must speak the mind of God in this mix of great opposition, while maintaining a godly attitude. Many are called but few are chosen.

Guard what you say and choose your words well, for a multitude of words can give rise to a multitude of curses and blessings. Choose well and live.

As the choicest fruits fall from a tree well nourished and maintained, so should the mouth speak the fruits of a mature heart.

It's needless to speak in the ear of a fool the wisdom of God lest he turn against you and mock your words.

Don't sweeten the words of Almighty God, for the Lord has already discerned the hardened heart.

If a life is abandoned to Jesus Christ she should have such an impact on others that, after a meeting, they will either look forward to meeting her again or hope to never meet again.

The heart of human can a depository of the essence of Jesus Christ and the mouth speaks the content of the heart if that one be in Christ Jesus.

A human cannot control every thought but the mouth will reveal the contents of the heart.

An open mind can be a blessing to many but the mouth reveals the heart of a person.

What Makes a Marriage Work?

A "sweetheart of a deal" is when God ordains the marriage of two high school sweethearts.

The relationships between male and female are limitless but too frequently enter areas guided primarily by the promise of sensual gratification and the results are not good in the long run for either party.

How can a man love a woman when he hates himself?

The friend of the bride is not always the friend of the bride groom---and life goes on.

Without the nurture of a marriage, days of wine and roses disappear quickly to be replaced by bread and briars, if bread can be found.

Most lovers think alike and share many things in common until payday.

A fiery kiss, a gentle caress is owned by no one, but loved by all and is free to everyone.

A raised clinched fist may promise victory, but is held fast by no one, and may fall in any direction.

A sensuous kiss may raise the dead, but a knife in the back will make sense of it all.

When someone says, "Hold on to your hat", you'd better be prepared to jump for your life.

A hug can enhance the promises of a good day and a kiss can seal the deal.

Let not the will of a wife exceed that of her husband lest a spirit of emasculation arise and confusion rule the roost.

If a man leads his family by Christ-like example, is he responsible for the conduct of his wife?

A family ruled equally by two or more is not a home of peace, and love is far off.

Days of wine and roses were never intended to last forever for they both fade with time and soon become a cherished memory.

The Word of God defines a man and his wife as one, but the power of hear-say and gossip can divide.

God preserves the lonely for Himself. But when the original matchmaker brings a pair together, a strong union is born.

The ways of a woman and her man are past finding out and few ever know the full truth.

One's partner can be an investment in another's future and a woman is far more valuable than a ruby, for God did not breathe the breath of life into a commodity but a living soul.

The swift stroke of a pen may end a troubled marriage but the residue may last forever. And life goes on.

A lazy wife and an unclean house will have no shortage of antagonists and her future will be doubtful.

A lazy man and a motivated wife cannot survive in a godly marriage and love will not last for the two are divided.

In a marriage, in-laws and outlaws have much in common; they want to drive but have no legal authority to sit in the driver's seat.

In some cultures men are allowed many wives and in some cultures men are protected from themselves by allowing only one.

Ordinarily, the hand that feeds an individual is the hand he guards most, but frequently this is the hand first bitten, for it's the hand least appreciated.

If an adulterous wife is encouraged by her weak, unloving husband, then her sin is somewhat minimized by his total indifference. Who has the greater sin?

A lonely maid and a distraught husband can love the night away but the devil comes at day break. And life goes on.

The lonely wife and devoted butler have much in common: Loneliness and revenge.

The pastor's wife and a foolish secretary may have two things in common: The desire for happiness and attention from the pastor. But the devil is in the pulpit.

A wise wife will feed her husband well and his home will be immaculate, but a foolish woman will feed herself and sleep alone.

Do not anger your spouse unnecessarily, for a slow death will not be easily detected.
Now, who is the wiser?

Those who tell a mate of past love affairs are seeking suicide by another's hand.

A nagging woman's words are like the unbroken circle of a wedding band: they never end.

A woman's unkempt emotions and a man's reckless bravado comprise the necessary ingredients for peace and calamity rules the day.

A man cannot love two women for long with ardor lest his candle burn out and his ardor diminish.

A husband's delight is in the wife of his youth if he did choose well, but the devil is in the details. His sleep will not be at ease without a wife of virtue.

Wisdom will choose a mate, God will consecrate both, and understanding will keep the peace.

A mate misunderstood is the rage of a marriage if one is not true. But they who seek wise counsel will find understanding, and those who seek wisdom will not share a bed with strangers.

Is the jealousy of one mate towards another a manifestation of love or the demonstration of one's insecurities?

A woman's ways should be the ways of righteousness and she should be able to follow a husband's example with confidence.

The wife of another sometimes seems more attractive to a man than his own because the "grass always appears greener," but the end is a fool's quest.

Is there an inherent competition between some husbands and wives based on their subconscious or conscious desires to equal each other in achievements?

Good Women and Bad Ones

A pretty face can be an invitation to a dream come true, or a calm before the storm.

A powdered face and painted lips may not signify true beauty, but it could be a diamond in the rough.

Late night bliss and early morning shame can dull a beautiful day.

The wife of one can be the mistress of many and the secret is known to none.

Women who allow others to look upon and treat them as commodities encourage such and invite more of the same. Let not such women think they will ever be free as long as their minds are not free.

It is said that a loose woman pursuing a man is like the fox chasing the hound and the end is seldom positive.

If a man is caught by a deceptive woman he is caught of his own free will and both are responsible.

The tragedy of seeking physical beauty is the need for constant affirmation. Inner beauty is an obvious and visible fact that need not be confirmed. The beauty is simply in being.

A woman of respect among her peers is second to none, and gains obtained in darkness will not last.

A harlot is known by her profession but who knows her end? Was Rahab not in the lineage of Jesus?

Drama is in the heart of a woman scorned, anger is her master, and seduction a means to an end.

Beware of the serpent under a warm blanket. Her kisses burn like fire and the sleeper sleeps on.

The mind of a woman on the prowl will not be denied and her seductions not a few.

Guile is the tool of a wayward woman, seduction her goal, and a foolish man she will find.

A darkened doorway and a corner lamp post promise joy for a moment but death is the companion of a foolish man. And life goes on.

Mincing steps and tingling bangles invite the lonely, but the devil may lurk in the closet.

One woman lives in the Governor's Mansion, the other woman lives in squalor. Why is one more esteemed than the other, for both may meet the same fate?

Physical beauty can be a harbinger of riches or the precursor of a downward spiral.

Can the beauty of a woman of leisure be assured over that of a woman of ordinary appeal? God judges all and is no respecter of persons.

The kisses of an adulterous wife are sweeter than honey, but destruction is her invisible companion.

Lust of the flesh is the weapon of choice for an adulterous woman and a wise man will not abide.

A woman on the prowl will not sleep for long, for her prey is on the move and she will not be denied.

A "sporting" woman and a man on the prowl have one thing in common, but daylight will separate the two.

The dim light of a doorway can hide a sinister smile on rouged lips. But after the fun, bright lights reveal the error made in haste.

Do not place your seed in the belly of a loose woman lest you pollute your good name.

Which woman should be more esteemed: the woman with spiritual values, a woman of exotic beauty, or the woman of stellar riches?

A woman's gentle voice and soft, soothing hands may bring comfort to a dying soul or may fool with a gullible mind.

A woman who aborts a child is guilty of murder two times; her spirit and her child.

A woman's heart is made to be wooed but her mind is another matter.

A woman of wisdom is a lady not easily persuaded by self glamorization and promises of those with dubious backgrounds who habitually prey on women of low self esteem. She is a lady of tact, of intelligence, and an ability to see beyond the obvious, for she knows where she is going and has already planned her route and time of arrival. She owes no man anything but the love of God and the reliance upon herself and her God.

Why do some cultures demand that women be quicker to come forth in shame after a certain act than men guilty of the same? Who bears the most guilt, the woman adulteress or the male partner?

A woman with a tough demeanor is a woman not easily seduced by some but may be more difficult to bring to the Lord.

A woman and drama is like a hand and glove.

55

A sultry voice, a fair complexion and a "come hither" look may inspire many to sin, and an addiction to death.

Is the woman's place in the family of mankind one of confident humility because of her second place in the creation of the genders? Who knows? But we do know woman is indispensible.

How to Get Rid of Hatred and Anger

A heart occupied by hate has no room for love, for every room in that heart is occupied by the relatives of anger and they all grow together.

The ego satisfied by anger is only sleeping for a season and will soon arise for another confrontation.

One's emotion and a volatile attitude will bring swift destruction to a seeker of pleasure.

An angry spirit knows no boundaries in the heat of battle.

Those who abuse others are seeking to justify their need for power.

An angry individual is a follower of the spirit of discord and violence is not far off.

God forgives the repentant but the heart of mankind may be a bitter repository of the misdeeds of others who have wronged him.

Judging others in anger is an exercise in futility, for the penalty one imposes on another is apt to return to the sender and the sender must bear the consequences of his own deeds.

To curse the light as some have done is to curse one's self, as the light is the source of all creation. He is the Light of the world, even Christ Jesus.

Who is the most dangerous, the quick tempered man or the man concealed in the dark?

A rock thrown from a hidden hand will return to the one who threw it and all will see.

Who can know the depth of hate but the hater, and he too will soon be devoured.

Carnal words spoken in anger and a defensive attitude are often manifestations of deeply held unresolved issues and destruction is close at hand.

Do not in anger charge another for fires you set, for it is unprofitable to you and will at some point burn you.

When a man places stumbling blocks in the path of another he invites retribution, but God says, 'Vengeance is mine and I will repay." And life goes on.

If your dog doesn't bark, don't beat him, for he may then bite the hand that feeds him.

Who is more trustworthy: a man with a bruised ego or an angry man with a gun?

Stealth is an invaluable tool in the hands of one under attack, but most volatile in the hands of an aggressor.

Beware of those who agree to disagree with you, for they may lay in wait for a more opportune time.

Everyone is accountable to someone who in some capacity acts as a caretaker, but who knows whether that caretaker will become a hateful dictator and your freedom of choice will become a thing of the past?

Who can save a violent man from the wrath of his deeds? For the error of his ways will confront him at the last minute of his life.

The lack of self esteem places one in a position to be a victim or victor. No one is safe from the rages of this angry person, and destruction is soon to come.

The visible things are things to which we can relate but there are other areas that humans are not privy to because their desire to "know" is self-serving, and their minds are unrestrained, and their intellect polluted with arrogance and rage.

Developing Mature Character and a Sterling Reputation

When we miss the opportunity to correct the wrongs of the past we strengthen those wrongs and cause greater harm to the others and hurts, which can last a lifetime.

Every day is another chance to right the wrongs of yesterday while giving someone else a chance to repent.

Peaceful contemplation will bring sweet results if combined with Godly determination.

A light in a corner is better than darkness in an auditorium.

Which is most revealing about you, your reputation or your credit report?

We are known in part by our reputation, but there is One who knows the rest of the story.

The whole of a human should not be determined by what he has but by the content of his character and his relationships with his fellowman.

A whole person is one whose spirit is not depleted and whose focus is on the realm of the impossible. For all things are possible in Christ.

One of the most painful experiences a human must bear is the fact that history never forgets.

History is made every day; those we have wronged witness to what we have sown and a tree is known by the fruit it bears.

A man's worth should not be based on his bank account but the depth of his morality.

One person is known for valor and another for integrity; which is preferred above the other?

One's reputation is spiritually relevant to one's future and is a determining factor in how one is received and judged by others.

The people whom we remember and who influence us most are not the people who constantly challenge us about godly things or about our attitude, but those who live their lives like the stars in the heavens: simply, uncomplicated, honest and unashamedly. These are the people that mold us. If you want to be of use to God, get rightly related to Jesus Christ and He'll use you unconsciously every minute of the day wherever you happen to be.

Let not the good say "I am wise," for his behavior will reveal the depth of his wisdom and all will know his name, for his reputation will precede him.

An elder who participates in the errors of the young cannot lead by example because respect is long gone.

Everyone has a price that can be measured in some form or fashion. What is your price?

Human emotions cover the entire spectrum of the human experience in the church of God for they are part of who we are as created by almighty God.

The expression of human emotions is expected and condoned by God, for they reveal the mind and heart of a person. Just control those precious emotions!

If a man learns to appreciate and respect the labor of those who went before him, he will have equal respect for those who labor right now.

Holiness is free to all who desire the best of which a human is capable. I am speaking on the spiritual level because the spirit was created before the physical and the spirit contains, manifests, and declares the physical and is eternal, without end.

The works of humans are many and varied, but few manifest the righteousness of the living God and have the testimony of Jesus Christ.

One's actions speak to the present state of mind and the heart is revealed by what one does.

An individual may well know a thing but will actually live what he believes.

Discerning Between True Morality and Immorality

Being deceived by one's own morality is like walking in darkness for you are blinded by your darkness.

Frequently the darkness in us is mirrored in others and we are displeased at what we see in that mirror.

Moral righteousness does not search for the wrong in others but seeks the good and accentuates the higher potential in them.

Morality is not determined by conversation but is manifested in the life one lives: righteousness in action.

Hidden shame is like a hostage taker: it has no pity or compassion. But the light of revelation will heal the bearer.

A darkened heart is a dying heart, for the heart of darkness, like vegetation, must have light in order for the essence of life to function in bringing and maintaining life. So does the heart require light from the originator of all light.

Holiness is not a goal as some define a goalkeeper, but a place in the spirit realm attained via righteousness.

Does the term "Equal justice for all," apply to everyone or only to all those in a certain category?

The weight of the conscience can be a burden too heavy to bear forever.

Sin often occurs in darkness and even occurs in the light, but God judges the day and the night.

Sin is ever present in the life of humans and the antidotes are few, but God knows them all and those that are His will not suffer loss.

Absence of proof in a matter is claimed to be a matter of perception, but the guilt will not go away.

"Signs of the time" are the normal manifestation of expected events and attitudes relevant to that particular time.

A society whose moral values are individually defined cannot survive as a nation and will ultimately be destroyed from within.

All who live outside the law justify the need of the law and those who administer the law confirm its need by the administration of decrees. And life goes on.

By what right does a person have the power to determine life or death over one weaker who has no power of retribution?

A dark night may seem like a lifetime when all one knows is darkness.

Morality is a thing of the past in the mind of many, but in due season the circle of time will bring all things back to the beginning and today's past will be tomorrow's beginning.

When I miss the chance to correct past errors in my life I strengthen the potential for present mistakes.

Are individuals identified by their sexual preference or does their sexual preference identify them?

If God created male and female to populate the earth and rule all that He has created, why would he ordain two of the same gender to engage in holy matrimony? Is God confused?

If everything produces after its own kind as the Holy Bible declares, then what do two of the same gender produce?

How can a human be free of himself after crucifying his flesh if he still consumes and relies on things of the flesh?

What humans fill their minds with is what they become in their flesh.

Those who listen to do His will are those who come to Him already devoted to the cause of Christ. They obey without contemplating.

A man or woman who physically joins his or her own sex to another of the same gender is not manifesting the Spirit or divine intentions of the living God, for God is not a lover of Himself but His creations in the flesh, joined for the express purpose of procreation.

When a nation can justify lambasting the Name of God in a public arena called the media in the name of free speech, everything is on the verge of moral collapse. Comedians, pop singers, and various other notables will one day realize that God is not asleep and will award every human according to his works.

Free speech is like poison wrapped in an ice cream sandwich; its good going down but wait until indigestion begins and the body slowly begins to disintegrate.

The depth of a human soul no one knows but fruits of the spirit will be known by all, for a tree is known by the fruit it bears.

A decline in morality signals a decline in the longevity of a nation.

There are cases in which both human choices are wrong. For example, what is the better move: helping someone to kill another or lying to protect someone who did?

If a man is only taught true knowledge by one who is knowledgeable, then how can an individual be taught the oracles of God by those who are not godly?

Woe to Christian leaders who lead the people of God to believe that all one has to do is seek and enjoy the good while ignoring the consequences of bad behavior. Lukewarm Christianity will fill the pews but ultimately will lead to destruction.

The irrelevance of the Church today is being criticized by many people throughout society and justifiably so. Churches all across this nation have become nothing more than social meeting halls, places for aspiring politicians to meet and greet the "people of God", places where various secular academicians meet to argue the existence of God and the list goes on. Many Biblical terms have been relegated to obscure, less potent and meaningless expressions to the joy of those who deny the deity of Jesus Christ. If Biblical prophecies are to be followed and believed, the world and this nation in particular are on a downward spiral to destruction.

These last days are the worst since the Flood, but the Word of God declares, "Where sin abounds grace does much more abound." The prophetic Word of God stands assured, and those who adhere to what the Spirit of God says will not suffer loss.

How to be Genuinely Successful

A successful end is not possible without a successful beginning.

Every person has a beginning, whether in secret or in the public arena, but his end may be known by many.

Quickly gained success can be like a hand filled with sand; it will quickly and easily slip away and your dream will become a glimmer of hope once again. And life goes on.

Immature excitement can cause one to jump into artificially bright lights and miss a clearly defined path to success.

Excitement based on a quick observation can dull the hard-fought wisdom gained from experience.

Successful endeavors invite successful people for they have things in common.

A feeling of worthlessness is vulnerable to those who wish to confirm your unworthiness.

The width and breath of heaven is known by none, but the bottomless pit bids one and all.

Habitual winners can be poor losers because they know not grace in defeat.

Success is defined by one's value system and what he believes. How blessed we as Christians are for we don't have that heavy responsibility; God has already made provisions for easy believing and He alone brings it to pass.

To settle for less is an affront to God for He expects more from a man than he thinks he is capable of giving. But God is the source of all and not we of our selves.

Delayed gratification can be an act of chivalry resulting in the death of an endeavor or a tactic waiting a more opportune time.

Many successes begin with a dream or a vision and end in the death of that vision or dream for lack of cultivation.

A wish is an unfulfilled desire without the conscious effort to bring it to pass.

Success is assured when a saint refuses to be defeated.

Today's preparation can be tomorrow's dream come true. Today's dreams and tomorrow's endeavors may signify the germination of success.

Passionate endeavors may attract the support of many experts in mind and body.

 To limit oneself is to proclaim defeat; there are no limits in those who believe, for '*All things are possible for them who believe*".

The highway is not always the best way. Roads to success usually begin on a low road.

A thing seen is no guarantee of safety and security is often cloaked in those shifting intangibles.

Winning is not an inevitable habit, but the results of right choosing at right times. Losing can become habitual as one becomes accustomed to making bad choices and is not encouraged because he never wins.

My greatest potential arises in the face of greatest risk.

Encouragement is the fuel of progress and pessimism, the tool of regression. They are in the hands of everyone according to their will.

Success is the goal of every endeavor and perseverance will bring home the bacon.

Endeavor is a matter of perception and longevity is to be determined, but true success speaks for itself.

Who is the victor, the one who is awarded the prize or the one who relents?

Temptation can be a test of a man's will to remain focused on his stated goal. If his mission is not stated, it is only a dream unfulfilled and a man can easily lose his way.

A man open to new opportunities will prosper in due season if he is not resign to despair.

Excuses are not just reasons to fail but words to justify a lack of movement forward.

Is contemplating an issue a waste of time or time spent in preparation?

Success is not always knowing what's over the hill but the willingness to go and succeeding in the journey.

Making Right Choices Determines your Destiny

So-called "deathbed confessions" are said by some to be the place and time when they will make their "calling and election sure," but why wait for a time, place, or circumstance when you know not what your end will be?

When we acknowledge the presence of the Spirit of God in the earth, we have arrived at a junction in our lives where a decision is required: We can accept God's gift of grace, repent and be saved, or we can tip our hat to Jesus, yet refuse to serve Him and, thus, be eternally lost. Devils acknowledge Him as savior but cannot live righteously; we can. We have a choice.

The heart holds much that is not revealed, but God knows the intentions and thoughts of men.

Two paths are open to humanity; one path is fraught with travail leading to destruction. The other is sealed with victory leading to eternal glory.

The heart of man determines one of two destinations and both have their reward.

It is absolutely necessary to give one a chance to act on the truth of God. This is an individual responsibility and must be left with that one alone. You cannot do that for him. It must be his own deliberate act, but the evangelical message ought to always lead to action.

The Christian worker must never forget that salvation is God's thought and is not man's thought. It is the great thought of God and not simply an experience. Experience is only the gateway by which salvation comes into conscious life.

Life does not consist of quantitative values, as many suppose, but life is the permission to exist given by a higher supreme power known as Jesus Christ: a challenge to emulate His person in word, deed, attitude and Spirit. These attributes constitute life lived at its best.

One cannot know others without first knowing one's self, lest confusion arise and the two become indistinguishable.

Never ask the advice of another about anything God has already revealed. If you seek differing advice, you'll nearly always side with Satan and your potential to be used in that instance will be lost because you will have become more carnal than spiritual.

The will is the motivator of every action of a person---born in the mind and resident in the heart.

To reach the fringes of outer space one must escape the natural hold of gravity. Likewise to reach the gates of heaven one must escape the natural hold of sin resident in every man, woman and child. Mankind must be an over comer.

God created humanity to be more than a commodity traded as goods for human consumption. Mankind was created in the express image of God as a witness to the divine power and creative ability of the Almighty God.

The saint and sinner travel two opposing roads ascribing to different domains and are responsible for their choice.

The young adult and the senior citizen view their world from different perspectives, and their happiness may be a far-distant dream fueled by their perspectives. Let them not be deceived, for both will face death.

The end of one thing is the beginning of another but we pray that the new is not an elevated continuation of the archaic.

It is best not to know some things in life for once a thing is known it often incurs a responsibility to conform to something related to what you have learned.

There is a place for the aged and a place for the young. A place for the old and a place for the new and then the end, and the cycle begin anew.

In living, following the path of least resistance does not require effort, only emotions and a degree of sentimentality.

Saving one's self from destruction can be as simple as making right choices.

A person's day begins with choices. Whether we walk, run, stand or fall we live by the choice we make. Know the whole of a matter.

Knowing you're not alone in the universe assures your destiny.

Standing still is not growth but affords one an opportunity to access what is needed to grow.

Lack of movement forward can be a blessing if one is not sure in which direction to move.

Winning hands are always accompanied by eyes that are fixed on the prize.

If a human believes all that he's heard, enters every door open before him and contemplates everything he sees, who could stand before him? And yet, the opportunity is ever present.

One's borders are ever changing but a few cannot be challenged.

Is it safer not surmising a thing or to stay in a dark place and never question? Some spend their whole lives in chains never knowing they have the key.

Things and people who are unfamiliar to us can challenge us to reach beyond the brink of the ordinary and become familiar with new opportunities, otherwise too far in the distant future to be of any immediate value.

Some dream of tomorrow and miss today's preparation for tomorrow.

All humans have three things in common: a timely birth, a life, however brief, and an unstoppable death. And God judges all.

Many paths lead to paradise as defined by some, but who knows when he has arrived and what is his ultimate destination?

Don't beat up on yourself over your emotions and feelings, but be concerned over your reactions to them, for you are responsible for those reactions and only you can determine outcomes.

The hope of glory is every Christian's goal, but few ever attain it.

He who begins a thing is not always destined to finish it. We are here for a season and who knows his ending?

"Burning midnight oil" may deplete the next day's supply, so where is the gain?

One's end is determined and set in the annals of eternity, but who among us knows the date or the hour?

The needs of a person are many and varied but the will of God is far greater.

The time for learning is right now, for tomorrow may be too late. What you learn right now will quite possibly prepare you for tomorrow's challenges.

If we knew our end, our enthusiasm would be less and our efforts not as strong---an easy prey for enemies.

The end of a thing can be a blessing or a curse, depending on the path one takes at that time. Like the sphinx, we can rise from the ashes or descend to a lower depth of destruction.

Are you afraid of your ability to do the right thing because of what others may say or is it easier to continue doing the wrong thing and win the applause of many?

Consequences of one's choices may be delayed but never denied, for the wages of sin is death.

Why do some worry, if they are assured of their immortality?

For most humans, the greatest fear is not what they can see, but what they cannot see or rationalize.

Why are so many people fearful and defensive about their coming death over which they have no control?

Every creation has a designated end. Whether heaven or hell. One's belief makes a difference. Humans can choose one destination or the other. But the final choice is God's.

The time for change is right now before someone reserves your space for tomorrow today.

Can a person think her way beyond where she is without seeing how to get there?

One's dreams will always be just that until the reality of action awakens the mind.

The term "date" has many connotations but one thing is often true: it is an opportunity to change direction in one's life.

Almighty God can heal anyone at anytime but one must desire healing to be healed, for God does not trespass on a man's will.

Circumstances frequently determine the outcome of a thing, but sometimes not, because some things are meant to be and cannot be avoided.

God gave humanity a wide berth in arranging and managing the natural affairs of this earth, with the ability to pick and choose according to one's desires. But to protect him from himself, God provides certain parameters beyond which no one can venture lest he completely destroy himself.

Take a long walk before dark, for it will afford a final opportunity to judge your day before the dark of night. Then plan what you will achieve the next day.

A man is born with a survival instinct that aids survival for a temporary period of time just as we exist temporarily. We did not come here to stay and neither do our skills enable it. We are only visiting this planet.

Overcoming the Hard Times

Is there no other way to survive other than "Hanging in there"? Why not just stand?

If you must sweat, then "Sweat the small stuff" rather than the large or you may be overwhelmed.

Don't fix that which is not broken and don't try to heal those who are not sick.

Suffering needlessly can become a habit. Some say we become a creature of our environment which will be manifested in the final output of our lives. We are what we have learned and identify with.

Faith untested is not faith but a promise unfulfilled.

Physical age is a gauge of one's place along life's path from birth to the grave, not necessarily a measure of the depth of one's wisdom.

The best things in life are not free, for death is often hidden in a costly meal.

Who can know the heart of a man except that man, and he is often unsure.

The promise of things to come keeps one motivated, a strong mind and a willing body can put the weak to shame, but faith in God will ultimately bring it to pass.

We live our lives in a crosshair, fired on from every side, but if we, by reason of choice, survive the onslaught, our passing this way will not have been in vain for we will have sown a seed for others.

Moving forward while ignoring past mistakes can allow a man to be attacked from the rear and his progress hampered.

Easy victories often bring easy defeats.

We die daily, but the promises of tomorrow strengthen our faith.

An enemy held close to a man's breast can afford one of two possibilities: be forewarned before he strikes or use his knowledge of your plans to enhance your victory.

The best place to conceal ones resources is in house of the enemy.

Why bet on what you don't hold in your hand and give another the advantage?

It is said that he who occupies the high ground rules not only his immediate surroundings but distant fronts are at his command. But for the worker in Christ, the dark valley below is where battles are fought and won.

Earth has no sorrows that heaven cannot heal.

Pain is the ultimate warning before a catastrophic event.

The "good old days" are just that; "good old days" and now cometh the new, for the old is no more than a fading memory.

Having a "good day" is a matter of perception based on one's perspective. Is the loss of the life of a dearly loved Christian who is terminally ill a good day?

Pray your days be free of worry, fears, disappointment and that all your enemies are at peace with you and that you have no apprehension of tomorrows.

Fear can be healthy but panic can cause a wall to collapse.

Those who implicitly trust God will not fear loneliness for they know that their life is completely wrapped up in the hand of Almighty God and they will never suffer loss.

It is the common ordinary, everyday things that offer the greatest potential for trouble in our lives. It is those familiar things that encourage us to relax and we become a target for the enemy.

Pain in the body, in the mind, or in another is a harbinger of things to come. Go to God with your pain.

Some spend inordinate amounts of time seeking an unseen enemy, but the enemy is within.

The source and identity of an unseen enemy must always begin at home and spread abroad.

A shot in the dark is not necessarily a wasted effort, for it is best to have tried and failed than to surrender without a fight.

Don't place your confidence in a promise for many will be your competitors and your victory doubtful.

Our faith must be continually tested lest we be as those drugged who fall asleep at the wheel. By all means, we must avoid life's ditches.

Who can escape the malice of others? Unless the likeminded band together, even the wise shall suffer harm and they all shall fall together.

We've heard the phrase "If you can't stand the heat, get out of the kitchen." But there are times when it is actually safer in the kitchen than in another place.

"The dawning of a brand new day" is sometimes a continuation of yesterday's agony.

"Know your enemy and your enemy can't harm you" It is always good to know when to hide.

Many obstacles may lie between a man and his goal, but a winner never truly loses and a loser rarely wins.

Is one better off not knowing a thing and being free from worry or knowing a thing and worrying over the complexities brought forth by that knowledge?

Intellectual curiosity without moral parameters can ultimately lead an individual to deep despair and destinations he is ill prepared to cope with.

Fear of physical death can cause one to adapt to positions that will ultimately cause greater pain than necessary.

I value what I possess most when I've lost what I always assumed I'd have forever.

One's enemy will be revealed when it is thought that he is defeated, helpless, and no longer a threat.

The life of the good is fraught with pain. What of the villain?

Every new day has its challenges and the night will declare a winner, but God will judge both.

A hasty retreat is better than a slow death.

A human is plagued by many things, both seen and unseen, but it is the unseen that offers the greatest challenge and can do the greatest eternal harm.

One cannot lawfully enter into certain realms beyond her earthly boundaries lest she be destroyed for possessing that which she has not earned the right to possess.

For the follower of Jesus Christ the greatest tests often come during the dark of night when visibility is limited and defenses are few, for we are children of the day and not the night. We don't do well in the darkness unless God be with us. Weeping may endure for a night, but joy comes in the morning.

A day in the life of a successful man is fraught with obstacles for obstacles are the motivators that success is borne of. Without which a vision will die on the vine for lack of a challenge.

The best time to move ahead is right now for there is no gain in waiting for tomorrow for tomorrow will have its own obstacles to overcome.

As my pain increases so does your grace abound even the more, and my misery, although great, is less an annoyance to my soul. Thy grace is ever present and helpful to me. I am so grateful to be the one worthy of this misery.

Often, time's tragedy is the strongest motivator for positive change in one's life because it causes him to rise above the pain of the tragedy.

The will to survive and a strong faith in almighty God's ability to guide one through the Red Sea are all one needs to get to the other side.

In the mind of a winner, obstacles are nothing more than stepping stones and the enemy nothing more than a shadow in the path to success.

Whether a person's days on earth are long or short, her life on earth is fraught with troubles and death is her ever-constant companion. We groan in these defective bodies, but someday all will be new.

We may see a goal and desire the prize but expect many obstacles to mar the way.

In these terrible last days God has a remnant in the midst of the ever increasing large crowds of people-pleasers and worshippers of idols.

In a happy-go-lucky society we forget that we live our lives in a dying environment, in the midst of a dying people, and, for many, the worst is yet to come.

The way of the cross is a hard and tedious road to walk but it is the only way to the inner court of our Lord and there are no short cuts or byways. It is the only way to heaven.

Never tell God how to solve a painful problem, who to speak to, when to do it, what to say, or what to do to bring to pass your agenda. He never told us to be our own little providence, but to just believe.

The Prime Importance of Prayer

The content of the heart is decidedly wicked but observation and prayer will reveal a matter.

Prayer energizes and revitalizes the spiritual component of the soul. It is the conduit of power between the Creator and originator of humanity and the essence of his being.

A night is long when the enemy is near, but the prayers of the righteous avail much.

A prayer half prayed is a step in the right direction but a prayer not prayed is no step at all.

People pray in many ways and at different times, but all must glorify Him who taught men to pray.

Almighty God has opened many channels of communications between Himself and His workers, but there is a direct line through His servants the prophets.

The effectual, fervent prayer of the righteous reveals a place of unspeakable joy in the spiritual realm that only they which are spiritual may enter. And the joy of the Lord is beyond comprehension to the glory of God in the highest.

Many hands in a pie do not assure good taste.

There are times to pray hard and keep your own counsel.

Prayer changes circumstances but, most importantly, it changes my relationship with God.

Sleep can come easily to an untroubled mind, but the sincere prayer of a righteous man can clear a troubled mind.

Prayer does change things, for it begins in the mind and then from the heart of the one praying and spreads abroad.

A discerning spirit is for the purpose of sincere intercession on behalf of another, not for our own piety.

Truth is frequently found after much deep contemplation and prayer far beyond one's own consciousness, buried deep within realms mortal mankind---realms he will never reach unless he has earned that rite of passage through love and devotion to the One and only living God.

No better time to pray than when one's heart is in a "tizzy."

Beware of the hand of strangers bearing gifts, for the gifts may have strings attached. But the believing, fervent prayer of the righteous avails much.

A wise man observes times and seasons and his prayerful attitudes will determine the height and depth of his successes.

Can a man teach the wisdom of Almighty God if he is not godly or can he discern the mind of God if he doesn't spend time in the presence of God?

A praying spirit and a grain of faith is fertile ground for a miracle.

The term often heard "praying on" someone is not scripturally sound and those who adhere to such practices risk the judgment of God. He alone is Judge and will ultimately determine guilt or innocence.

Everyone has a beginning and an ending. Pray they are not too close together.

A praying worker in Christ is an overcoming worker in Christ, and all they do shall prosper and bear much fruit.

The wiles of Satan are far beyond man's comprehension and ability to control, yet his defeat is assured by the simplest acts of man: prayer.

Prayer does change things. It starts in the heart of the one who is praying and spreads abroad.

One can speak to God at any moment in time and accept the promises of God at will, but will he?

What is the Power of Thanksgiving and Praise?

The heart of God is touched by praises and the prayers of His saints will not be unheard.

We often sing the praises of Zion, and then we deny the existence of the Father.

A pretty face does not constitute a beautiful person anymore than a buffed body constitutes a healthy individual.

All things originate from within the spirit of an individual and are manifested externally in numerous ways.

Songs of praise will illuminate the spirits of other and God is glorified by our testimonies.

Time and space are inherent gifts to humanity, for every man, woman, and child are allocated time and space to win souls for Christ and glorify God.

In singing songs of praise and adoration The Most High God will soon drive away a spirit of dread and your joy will be complete.

Praises to God will lighten the heaviest load and the dark of night will soon pass.

There are two kinds of spirits residing within mankind and only one will have dominance.

He speaks to all creation in languages they all understand and yet none are confused and all praise Him in their individual splendor and He is glorified.

To be fully appreciative of a good day one must have experienced and remember a bad day.

We do all things godly after the manner of men and certain parameters constrain us greatly, but the Spirit of God takes man beyond the brink imposed by earth, and God is glorified.

Songs of praise to God may not be praises to God at all but to the leader of the band.

The most important day of your life is today, for tomorrow may never come. He who moves now will often catch the blessings of that moment in time which will never return.

My God, most worthy, almighty, holy God, bless thy Name and may all men glorify thee. I lift up the Name of Jesus and as I sit here and offer up praises to you my heart is full of gladness and rich with the joy of being in your presence right now and I offer this testimony of praises to you, the living God and I would that all who read these few lines are blessed and healed of their many infirmities. In Jesus' Name, Amen.

May the life I live be a living testament to the glory of the living God in my life and a witness to His ever presence in my life and what He can do for an apt sinner such as I.

He who has a heart of thanksgiving will not covet the possessions of another but rejoice in all things godly.

The mind of God contains all things that exist pertaining to humanity and no one can entertain these glories lest he become as God and God has declared "I will not share my glory with another." Mankind's existence is justified and qualified by his willingness to worship and glorify Jesus Christ to the honor of the living Almighty God.

God reveals to man the knowledge and understanding necessary to offer up sacrifices of praises to Himself and to perpetuate the godly species on the earth. Carnal knowledge is detrimental to the survival of sinful, arrogant, and prideful mankind.

The praises of Almighty God emanate from the mind of the man or woman of God, feed the Spirit of God within a man, and lift the heart to the throne of God.

How does a Christian Grow?

To be raised in Christ makes a person heaven bound.

The essence of a spiritual man can be substantiated to the extent that this mortal man is able to contain the person of Almighty God and live.

A bed for resting, a seat for sitting, a knee for bowing, an eye for seeing and an ear for hearing, but the soul is designed for God.

If contemporary practices and beliefs are any indication, there are two kinds of Christians: Bible-believing Christians and self-defined Christians. Which category defines you?

Humility is not the manifestation of one's fears, but the foundation on which to build a bastion of faith leading to victory over an oppressor of any sort, for that which is spiritual is of the Spirit. Where sin abounds, grace much more abounds and the might of God will always be victorious in the hands of a soldier for the Lord.

We read some things in the Bible over and over and they mean nothing to us, then all of a sudden we see what God means because in some odd or particular way we have obeyed God, and instantly His nature is revealed to us. "All the promises of God in Him are yea, and in Him Amen." The "yea" must be born of obedience.

The reason some of us are such poor specimens of Christianity is because we have no Almighty Christ. We mouth Christian words and ideals, but there is no abandonment to Jesus Christ. We speak of His glory and His saving grace and even His ability to deliver, but we have no abandonment to Him.

Adults can be seen as children who have attained the stage of maturation in which developmental capacities have evolved into the abilities to make sound, rational, and godly decisions.

Other than fervent, effectual prayer, the most effective motivators in the worker's life is one's enemies, for they tend to drive the worker to seek the favor of God so much the more.

The mind of angels inhabit one dimension. The mind of God's ministers and teacher s reveal another dimension, His prophets and musicians yet another. All are subject to His will, for all serve the Most High and He shares with whom He pleases.

The needs of an individual are an opportunity for growth in many areas of life because God expects more of him than any other creation.

Time is an element that exists for every Christian. As a reference point it separates the beginning and end of a person's endeavors in measuring progress. But only God knows the date and hour.

As humility is the first step down in the death (spiritual) of the worker in Christ, so obedience is the first step upward, for attitude determines ones altitude in Christ.

After a season of preparation, following Christ is not so much a conscious effort as an attitude because Christ has already occupied the willing mind and His Spirit is one with the follower.

If the heart of a human is filled with the Spirit of Christ, what he speaks will be in the Spirit of God and there will be no condemnation.

On earth, the work of God's servants is never done, for when the body tires there exists a supernatural source of replenishment and the worker marches on into eternity.

Seeing with the eye is perceiving, seeing with the Spirit is knowing, and believing with the heart is being one in Christ to the glory of God.

Learning the rules of living is always being taught in the Potter's House.

My attitude toward life will determine my altitude in Christ.

My soul is ever changing and there should be a corresponding change in my mind lest I have lost my focus and I have become a prisoner of stagnation.

Self-proclaimed martyrs are of no use to God. He wants you to be a living sacrifice, to allow Him to have all your powers that have been saved and sanctified through Jesus. This is the only thing that is acceptable to God.

A broken heart is hard to mend if the owner refuses to fight the good fight of faith and let God have His way.

There are two paths in a man of God; one path to be traversed by the Lord and one path to be traversed by humanity (Poured out wine and broken bread). Who can abide in this place reserved for those who are truly abandoned to Jesus Christ?

Every sin must be revisited with godly repentance made from a sincere heart before one can proceed to sanctification.

When one understands the nature of godly ways and strives to observe them, she has a covenant obligation to obey in all things biblical.

Living a godly life in Christ will bring eternal results, for a fruit does not fall far from the tree.

The natural life is not spiritual and can only be made spiritual by sacrifice. If you and I don't make a determined effort to sacrifice our natural life, the supernatural cannot become natural in us. There are no short cuts here; each one of us has that capability in our own hands and it's not a question of praying but of doing.

God introduces us to many things in the natural so that we may know what He expects us to sacrifice naturally for the supernatural. He says let everyone be fully persuaded in his own mind whether he will follow Him.

When we accept His invitation to take up our cross and follow Him we have no idea what that cross will be. But we are already convinced that He will help us through His grace and that cross will never be more than we can bear.

Those whose strides are a daily exercise in faith will attain a crown if they faint not, for they have the favor of God.

Do what Jesus did, when He did it (circumstances), with the faith that Jesus had and get the same results that Jesus did.

Checking the Power of Greed

Our needs are many and varied, and the need to grasp rather than give is an ever growing and gnawing element of our nature. But giving from one's heart can go a long way in taming that spirit of greed.

The more self-centered you become the less like Christ you are and the less likely you are to be godly, because most of your energy is focused on self gratification, and seeking the approval of others. Then unfulfilled needs are manifested in frustration and anger

The heart determines one's fate. Its destination is determined by no man, but all can influence it.

Truth is not partial to any, but lies have their favorites.

Is the media the voice of the masses or the darling of capitalism? And the giant sleeps on.

Money is the opiate of capitalism. Christian capitalists cannot be addicted to more of the same.

Capitalism promotes and breeds success. The fallout is predictable, for some get left behind. Where is the winner, who is the loser? Many know but few will tell.

An act of retribution in the mind of many against the darlings of capitalism will only spawn a greater addiction to the lure of money, for there is profit to be made in warfare and welfare.

A man and his money can be an institution unto himself---a self regulated island of refuge basking in a deceptive sense of security.

How can one manage more of things hoped for tomorrow when her hands are filled with the substance of today?

Gluttony can be defined as two hands full and no way to retrieve that which falls from one of the hands.

Men cannot step upward when their attention is focused on what they have to leave behind.

A hand in the pocket is an advantage as long as it's not your pocket.

If a man claims his goal is to protect the poor, why does he yet defraud so many?

Be careful who pays your rent; in some cultures it is said that "He who has the money holds the reins".

A wealthy man's money is his glory and his heaven is his own making and, beyond that, he will not enter in.

Riches and bravado often go hand in hand, but wisdom is afar off.

Keep your distance from the greedy lest they steal the ground you stand on.

A man of substance's mind is apt to be filled with just that and the depth of his mind can be measured in profits and losses. Where is his glory?

Those who pursue heaven on earth may be satisfied with the instant gratification of living a life free of great challenges. But, ultimately, will fall far short.

The rich one in Christ and the rich one who knows not Christ are on opposite sides of the spectrum for one is seeking how he can please God and the other how he can keep his riches.

No individual can make what is impure pure, for what is presented as such is detrimental to all. The glory of God is not in the carnal quest and the love of money is the root of all evil.

In the ungodly mind, curiosity is substituted for wisdom, and cleverness is of paramount importance, for it inflates the ego and the promise of great wealth is the driving force. However, the end will not justify the means, and the arm of almighty God is stretched out still.

If you were required by law to make an immediate choice, which would you choose: the promise of total freedom from financial problems for life or the promise of eternal worship before God's throne?

The media is an ever-present greedy conglomerate that is focused on this moment in time because Wall Street won't wait for tomorrow and many will suffer loss, even loss of life.

The media's often-sensational proclamation of the minority's economic plight sells copy which is supported by corporate America's purchase of advertising, as well as sensational writing by certain flamboyant writers. But who helps the minority?

A nation of plenty gained by greed on the backs of slaves will soon be consumed by the greedy and the top will suddenly drop off and those beneath will suddenly rise above.

Corporate greed and the nation that condones it will soon be consumed from within and great will be the fall of it. The chickens are coming home to roost and are arriving daily.

Money has not a conscience and favors no one in particular, but he who gains riches by stealth will lose it by stealth and all will know their shame.

The freedom of many is threatened by the Bosses of the rich and powerful, but the One who directs the affairs of all will in time reveal His ultimate plan for survival and the Bosses will be no more.

What is God like?

One of the biggest challenges facing the Christian churches today is the tendency to rationalize and reduce to an academic explanation the existence of the supernatural creator who is in control of everything and to whom everyone in the universe answers.

A king is not a king without subjects but the King of glory is self perpetuating and His subjects eternal.

Jesus is the lifeline to which every human should attach himself but few ever find it.

The days of our lives are few and the dark of night many, but the light of God illuminates them all.

Truth is a never ending body of God's thoughts beginning in creation and extending into eternity. No human can understand more than a fraction of this truth and God reveals it to whom He will.

Who can know the mind of God but those who are His and do His will, for those who do His will have His Spirit and they are one.

The thoughts of humanity are after-thoughts of God for He is first and all thought exists in Him originally.

What is light but the Word of God made visible to men? What is power but the accumulated knowledge of God concentrated for a specific purpose at a given time in space? What are the eyes of God but the living, thriving, breathing, all knowing Creator of the universe reacting to every action and reaction in a controlled manner?

Many things cannot be changed, have no obvious answer and most of life is ever perplexing. But the depth of love and hate is far beyond the understanding of mortal mankind. Almighty God has shed a far deeper love for us and an equally greater disdain for sin. Where sin abounds grace much more abounds.

Brighter is the light of God than any other illumination and darker is the veil of darkness for it is equal in objectivity, but where sin abounds grace much more abounds.

The thoughts of God are not as rare as some suppose, but filtered by His Spirit to ensure that only the wise will receive them, for from he who receives much, much is expected.

The attention of mankind lasts but a moment and is soon forgotten. But the attention of God lasts an eternity and, unlike human attentions, is never cast aside for a moment of pleasure.

The power of the king is in his pen and his signet. The power of Almighty God requires neither, and sustains them both and will never be deposed.

Living in the light as God is the light requires much adapting to things of the light unseen with the natural eye. But Almighty God is a discerner of the intentions and thoughts of humanity.

Uncontrolled emotions can lead to rash promises. Jesus displayed the full range of emotions but was under control.

It's not the will of God that any should perish; God would find it a great delight if all lived a holy life to the glory of Christ.

The Word of God is neither sweet nor bitter, hot, nor cold, but comes down on the side of righteousness which cannot be categorized just as Almighty God cannot be categorized. But stands alone unto Himself. So does righteousness, a manifestation of holiness.

To know the mind of Christ one must make a conscious effort to know Him in the beauty of holiness and to do His divine will to the glory of Almighty God.

Most people are known by name, address and social status, but few know their hearts and even less know their intentions, but according to the Word of God, God is not mocked and every man will reap what he has sown.

God has absolutely no limitations, period. No human being should wish they knew all things. God has declared He would not share His glory with another.

The love of God rests upon every creation, for nothing was made that He didn't create. But only the creature made in His image was able to break His heart.

God has allowed mankind to reign over all living things on earth, but God Almighty maintains the essence of all living matter created by Him and, without Him, nothing was created that did appear.

In the kingdoms of men, a king must have subjects to rule over to be considered, thought of and respected as a king. The living God is not subject to any such needs and limitations for He alone creates His subjects and rules over them with a rod of iron and His mercy endures forever. He alone is King of Kings.

"Political correctness" is a popular secular term that obviously attempts to deny the righteousness of almighty God in preference to a god that accepts everyone and everything for the sake of harmony among all. Peace and harmony among all people and nations will never be achieved because of mankind's sinful nature and his unwillingness to adhere to the principles of a holy, righteous God that he cannot understand or manipulate.

God sees all, knows all, judges all and saves all who are His, yet who knows the time of their departure?

Jesus rarely comes when, or from the direction we expect Him to show up. He seldom enters into the situations we expect Him to appear. But He does show up in the most illogical situations and times. He frequently does not come through the front door, or even through a window. But know for sure He will come, and He alone will determine when and how.

God is a friend to the friendless, a father to the fatherless, a physician to the sick, and a revealer of truth to the gossiper.

Avoiding Foolish Excesses

Easy, sensual gratification can promote laziness but the motivation to achieve a higher level of enrichment can lead to inner completion and spiritual satisfaction.

Entertainment defined by some may seem harmless enough, but, to another, is a means to a horrible demise.

Alcohol can stymie the will and reveal the content of a darkened heart, and the road is always downhill.

In the halls of darkness lie many secrets but the light of God reveals them all at an appropriate time.

Three hours of merriment and one hour of free flowing wine may dull the best minds and the foolishness it causes is not remembered.

A cunning woman with crimson lips and a little wine can dethrone a king.

Excitement can be revived by a sensuous kiss, but the price can be self-destructive.

The carnal person is earth bound and all earth's pleasures define his estrangement from God.

Popularity is the carnal mind's key to survival without which the carnal soul would perish for lack of attention from those who promise titillation of the mind.

Titillation of the body is the opiate of the mind. It focuses on instant gratification without acknowledging the personal and global consequences.

A drink to seal a deal sounds good but the devil is in the second round.

A thrill may last but a second--- a minute at most, and the memory for a lifetime, but the consequences may last through the third and fourth generations.

A loving hand is security not easily found, but a hand held tight en route to a tryst will soon be loosed, for its aim is centered in lust.

Instructing a drunken man is like flailing against the wind; it's an exercise in futility.

Riches, friends, and frivolity can be lethal in the hands of one without understanding.

Soothing words and soft music will heal a broken spirit but death is in the drink.

He who starts the day with an alcoholic drink will, most likely end the day drunk before the night is through.

Many who spend a night of bliss and stolen kisses will face the dawn in fast retreat, for the light of day reveals all flaws in the flesh.

Wretched is the human who is known for his sins.

An hour of stolen bliss in the arms of another person's spouse might foretell a less than blissful trip into eternity.

Don't sign your death warrant in the form of a check for the services of a gigolo or a lady of the night.

It's not always the foolish that succumb to the joys of the midnight tryst, but all fight the battle and temptation has no favorite sons or daughters.

Becoming a Giver, not a Taker

If you are generous and seek the good in others then the good in you will be manifested in godly humility---not piety but unconsciously doing the will of Almighty God.

Those who give to the needy in season will reap a harvest in due season if love was the motivator for giving.

Money can relieve the heaviest burden, feed a hungry mouth, give drink to a thirsty child, but it can also wrongly entice a child or destroy an unborn fetus.

A day's labor is just one installment in the odyssey of a poor man and the band plays on.

Do ignorance, illegitimacy and rap music glamorize poverty?

To what extent do those who proclaim the existence of poverty benefit from the proclamation of poverty?

Feeding a hungry child is an investment in the future but who knows what will be the reward? Great trees often come from small seedlings planted in fertile soil.

The life you save may be your own when the life of others is your first priority.

Lessons in giving are better caught than taught.

Knowledge is dangerous in the hands of a greedy man, but wisdom will save his soul.

Money, greed and lust are never lonely for friends and many heed their call.

One is lustful and the other is greedy; which is the worst of the two? Are not all humans desirous of more?

Who is the worse of the two, the one who stole the food or the one who consumed it?

A swarming horde of locusts on a field of corn eat their fill and die: so will devourers of the works of the poor have their fill and die in their place.

Habits of the greedy are hard to break but the Word of God stands sure: "I will repay," says the Lord God Almighty.

An individual taught to beg will never look beyond the hands that feed him, for his view of himself is that of a beggar.

Those who kiss and tell will sell to the highest bidder for money is their first love.

Poverty is sometimes perpetuated by those who proclaim its existence without encouraging personal accountability.

If a merchant is a seller of goods and the theologian a preacher of the Gospel, by what titles are the perpetuators of poverty known?

A helping hand is a blessing if the goal is God's will, but a curse if the goal is to make you a debtor.

Family and Rearing Kids

The whims of children are never satisfied and neither can be, for children are incapable of thinking like responsible adults.

Parents who fear their children will be tomorrow's casualties.

A mother's love for her son is equal to none, and discipline taught from the womb can save a soul.

Every male has a donor but fathers are few.

Houses are built by hand, home by hands from the heart and occupied by the spirit of God in love.

A father's love for his daughter is second to none and a mother's son is never guilty.

A baby's cry can awaken the dead and a mother's work is never done.

The arrival of a new life is announced by a crying babe and the departure of the old is announced by the weeping of widow or widower.

Who can know the heart of a child but a mother; who can see beyond the obvious, but a mother? A mother's love is beyond comparison and yet, is often the most abused by those she loves most.

Better to hold a tiger by its tail than share a house with an angry woman or a rebellious child.

A family of seven may overflow with opposing agendas while the enemy lives within, but with the Spirit of Christ, the seven will soon be one.

A destructive spirit can exist in the midst of a wayward child; a bitter parent and love is soon a thing of the past.

The family that prays together stays together but the enemy lies within and is stealthy.

The heart of a child is given to folly and a wayward spirit his companion, but wise, godly correction will save the soul from death.

A loving mom is gracious, compassionate, loving, kind and a bastion of understanding (and gullible to a fault).

It is said that "Every house is not a home", but sometimes it's the only place we have.

A cuddly baby can endear a mother's love but a jealous father can kill the joy.

Hunger is a strong motivator for a mother in need and providing for her kids knows no bounds.

Who can know whether a child at birth will be a saint or a sinner?

One's home is where his heart is and if a man has no heart, he has no loving home.

Are you sure the "apple of your eye" is not a lemon in disguise? In time God will reveal the true identity, for a fruit does not fall far from the tree.

Vulgarity and a low aptitude are not necessarily synonymous but speak to the environment from which one comes and a lack of decorum.

Everyone is haunted by something, as a prodigal child is haunted by the love of the mother. What are you haunted by?

A wise woman has many faces and wears many hats but she manages her children well; her husband adores her, and the angels of the Lord surround her.

A male child cannot benefit from the wisdom and understanding gained from a male model if the model is not present or does not exist. A woman cannot teach a boy child to be a man, and to emulate a female is not what Almighty God intended.

A child unsupervised is a catastrophe in the making. Few will understand its origin, but many will suffer.

Political correctness has marred the separation between the sexes and many young minds are perplexed and confused.

The life of a parent can perpetuate the grief of their children, and in the halls of shame there is much remorse.

Wise is the woman who does not compete with her daughter for her husband's attention.

Is a female a "mother" because of her ability to give birth or is she a "mother" based on societies' definition of what a mother is or should be?

Why is a child sometimes influenced more in daily behavior by the mother than the father? Is it because the mother reinforces her instructions with, "Just wait til your father gets home!"?

Who knows the heart of a child like a mother, for frequently one mirrors the other?

An infant knows its mother and is haunted by her in her absence.

Relationship with God

From birth to the grave a man is in a spiritual free fall until he is rescued by the presence of God in his life.

Can humans adequately define themselves with the knowledge God has given them about themselves?

How can a man define himself as anything less than a representation of the one who created him without admitting that there is a power greater than himself?

Let not any man or woman say, "I didn't know!" at the last trump of God, for His presence and manifestation is all around: in every green tree, on every winged creature, in every chirping beetle, and on the face of every child. It is manifested on the face of the rainbow and in the billowing clouds before a storm.

"That old ship of Zion" has encouraged countless thousands to come to the Lord during camp meetings, revivals and church meetings down through the centuries. Many did not "get on board," much to the sorrow of others who accepted that plea. How about you?

There comes a time in some people's lives when they are consciously aware of a need for something beyond their rational explanation or reasoning. Alcohol, narcotics, gambling, carnal pursuits or traversing the planet cannot scratch that invisible itch and in the passage of time the universal King of Kings will be revealed to you and you will thirst no more.

A man has many rites of passage to many places but only one is guaranteed because of the redeeming death of Jesus.

If you agree with God's purpose for your life, He will explore every open door for you and you will become aware of many choices and seek the best.

The discipline of silence in the life of a saint is one of necessity as the saint grows into maturity. The voice of the Shepherd is not mute, but He wants to know "Can I trust you in my silence?" Learn to wait for that still small voice to guide you.

When I learn to relate everything in my life to the life of Christ in me everything suddenly becomes crystal clear and I see things not seen before because I was blinded not by light but the darkness in me.

Be ever ready at all times for the surprise visit of God in your life. He may not come in one direction or the other, but He will come and He will come when least expected. Just know that He is coming.

When God speaks, to many of us, it's like hearing a voice in a barrel. We know that we heard something but we dare not acknowledge it as the voice of God, because then we would have to do something in response to the voice and that, of course, we're not ready for.

Every now and then God will censure me and finding nothing to chastise me for, will begin revealing direction of which I knew nothing, as if to get me to another place before the sun sets. I become more aware of His plans in my life and the life of others than ever before. My will is to obey.

Whenever I am in the midst of doing business for the Lord I must do so in view of His will for me at that time and it is His will that I must always stand behind and let Him lead, and I must follow.

A man's heart is not subject to the understanding of any human, for it is too complex and full of mysteries to be discerned by any but almighty God.

Don't expect to know God unless you are familiar with His attributes.

How can a human know his end except he consult a higher power than he? And one says there is no God, then why is he so afraid to die?

Never worship that which is less stately than you, or you may become your own little providence.

Those who fear the Lord have a refuge that cannot be overrun, for they know Him who is invincible.

A secret is only as secure as the heart of the one who knows the secret, and who knows the heart of an individual but God?

There is a spirit of mankind attainable through hypnosis, deep meditation or recanting various mantras, but these have their limits because entering into the Spiritual realms of the Living God is far beyond and above hypnosis and anything ever envisioned by anything or anyone He created and He did create all things and He has said He will not share his glory with another.

The man or woman who acknowledges his or her own creation by the One and only universal Creator is beginning to know a truth often contested but never proven void of truth.

All of God's creations were created in an orderly fashion. That which was created in God's image has more glory than that which was not. Every human creation is superior among its kind to all other species. Only humans can know God personally.

The living God serenades His children through His Word for He soothes them with words of comfort and assurance. And they sleep and rest in a peace that passes all understanding.

Can a man know the heart of his woman unless she tells him? Who knows God's expectations unless they ask Him? Who knows what the dawning of a new day will bring but that one who stands ready for the challenge?

We see many things but gaze upon that which amazes and encourages us to move forward.

The Bible declares that a thousand years is but one day in the Lord, so we have no need to hurry but for one thing and that is seeking Jesus while He may be found.

When you hear the voice of God, move. Do not procrastinate. Go quickly, as opposed to wrestling with that thing and coming down on the side of Satan.

Humanity has been created to glorify God in the highest and one of his physical attributes is the ability to sing in harmony with the music produced by the minstrel as various instruments are manipulated. This, in turn, arouses the spirit within man to receive what God has to say to His children. There exists a close relationship between the OT Prophets and the presence of the minstrel.

We are often alienated---like two people passing in the night. We succumb to our desire to seduce or be seduced out of our need to be recognized because our self-esteem has, perhaps, become damaged beyond repair. But God is able to reach down beneath the lowest level and save us from ourselves.

There is a space in time not discerned by human consciousness and not readily explained by human rationale but eternal in the heavens where one can discern the mind of God in an extended but limited moment in time.

A human being cannot know the mind of God beyond that which is common to mankind, and that to a limited degree, according to his holiness and the divine will of God.

When one speculates on the divinity and manifestations of Almighty God he will come down on the side of Satan almost every time.

No man can know that which is not common to man except the Lord reveal it to him but, in the end, it is God who determines the truth of a matter.

Every person's eventual destination is the grave but his final destination is a matter of faith in Him who rose from the dead to give everlasting life.

Almighty God will not show more than what is common to a human being, even those to whom He chooses to speak directly via His Spirit. For the human mind can only sustain a fragment of God's essence, and there are things not lawful to be known by a human.

A soldier for the Lord has no business trying to protect the reputation and witness of Jesus Christ. He is not equipped to do so. What he has to protect is himself from himself, for the Word of God is power unto itself and no man can offer up adequate supernatural protection. We are to be witnesses to Jesus, not protectors.

'If I be lifted up, I'll draw all men unto me." My job is not to be my own little Holy Ghost, Jr. but a witness for the Lord in every circumstance. In every opportunity let my light shine before others.

When a soldier for the Lord drifts into darkness, everything spiritual becomes as dark as night, but when he gets back into the light of God, everything becomes as clear as crystal.

"Let that mind be in you which was in Christ Jesus." If I allow my mind to be filled by the Spirit of God, supernaturally wonderful manifestations of the presence of the living God will transform many lives into vessels of honor.

When we know and appreciate the attributes of a loved one because we have spent considerable time in their presence, we see no need to argue or defend their reputation or their existence in our lives. The fact that they are real to us is sufficient enough for us to love them the more. Why not the same for our Lord and Savior Jesus Christ?

A human must always ascend to a place higher than himself to find God, for God will always be found at a place higher than the created for He is the creator.

Are not the things of God holy unto all that He shares them with?

God speaks to all but only those who are His will hear his voice.

God's strides are long and constant and not many can stride with Him, but He strengthens those who will.

In spite of all the relationships we have and develop there is only your personal relationship to a personal Redeemer and Lord that really matters. Let everything else go and fall along the way, but maintain that one relationship at all cost and God will fulfill His purpose through your life.

Every human being was and is in need of constant replenishing and the only one with the ability to meet that constant need is the one who created humanity.

Persevere: Never, ever give up

Too much celebrating at the start of a program may reduce the available perseverance needed to complete the job.

A human will not and cannot run beyond his capability. His capability has been determined by many factors before he began his run, many of which he himself instituted. However, we must not place unnecessary limitations upon ourselves.

A human without hope is defeated before she starts.

When bodily fatigue is maximized, an individual's natural defenses are minimized.

Much knowledge without understanding is burdensome and will tax the spirit. We must persevere to understand that which we have heard and implement it in our lives.

Persistent desires and a strong determination to achieve a goal will result in success.

Who is capable of achieving the most, the person who diligently works towards his own goal or the one whose goal was given to him?

If a human will abide in his calling persistently he can do supernaturally marvelous things in Christ for he will have made himself an available channel to be used by the Spirit of God to perform the Lord's will on earth.

A calm mind is a most potent mind for it is not weakened by the loss of energy and the brain is not fatigued. Be calm, yet persevering.

Those who are super-efficient often generate unreasonable expectations in the minds of others. But does this mean that the persevering should ease up?

Patience, time, wisdom and persistence all speak the same thing to a godly man or woman: work and wait!

To Make you Think

If the law is for the lawless, why must the innocent suffer for the misdeeds of the lawless?

Who is incarcerated, the one behind the bars, or the one holding the keys?

Is learning a curse, a blessing, or an escape from reality?

Does a blacker page make a white page whiter or a whiter page make black page blacker?

Is white paint truly a paint absent of colors or only a paint waiting to be identified by the integration of color and thus, no longer a white paint?

Is the stay-at-home mother more esteemed than the nursing mother?

Who can guarantee the fruitful end of any man?

Can he that is dead live again?

Hidden knowledge can be a heavy burden so it is best that some things are never known.

By what right do the strong have the mastery over the weak?

A horse would seem more appropriate than a donkey to communicate strength because the reputation of a horse is of power, the donkey, of stubbornness.

Do you consider your reality the totality of human experience, or are you trying to live someone else's reality?

The end of a thing is the beginning of another and nothing is without precedent.

A walk in the rain is favored by some, but a chilled body is sought by none.

To what extent is a man free, and what defines freedom?

To what extent does a man love the Christian God?

Never place all your eggs in one basket or you may break the eggs and ruin your basket.

Which is best: to know a thing and face destruction or not to know a thing and face destruction?

Can a man defeat his enemy when he does not know his own strength?

Night and day have one thing in common; they are both elements of time and consequently are limited in duration.

Is the presence of vast numbers of ignored, poverty-stricken people an unstated benefit to a thriving global economy to be used as a ready source of manpower in case there is war?

What is real to a human but that which is his reality?

Is the healthy body of more value than the body bruised by war zone explosions? For both have hearts made of flesh.

How can we know others when we do not know ourselves? And the beat goes on.

If sunshine promotes a healthy body and spiritual truth promotes a healthy mind and spirit, which is esteemed the more?

What are the limits of one human's knowledge?

How far into time can a person see? When she sees beyond his comprehension of mortal things she is beyond herself for there are areas where humans are not allowed to comprehend or view for their own good and safety.

Is the mind of a human a reflection of who he is or a reflection of his surroundings?

Is a person's creativity reflected by her attitude or her attitude reflected by her creativity?

If two people are one, as in the case of a married couple, then why is it fair to sue one and not the other?

When God said He would not share His glory with another was He referring to a mortal man or another god competing with Him and presenting itself as God?

Who can save a human from himself if he has not the will to live?

Who is worthy of more honor, the person who dies for Christ or the one who brings many to Christ?

Which is closer to the heart of a child, the mother who nurtures or the father who provides?

Which deserves the greater honor, you or the One who created and sustains you?

Whom does God love more, the one who professes Jesus as the Son of the living God, or the one who teaches others that Jesus is the Son of The living God?

Is half a godly truth from a Biblical perspective preferred over no truth at all from a Biblical perspective?

Is an individual capable of determining what is best for him and his or is that capability best left in the hand of strangers?

Do I have the right to determine your fate if I provide your monetary support?

Who is best able to make rational decisions relating to his upkeep: the employed man because of her positive thinking of herself, or the unemployed because of her freedom from worry over day to day needs?

Is honesty always desired, even when one is about to lose a long sought after goal?

Is a good sense of humor always appropriate in every situation?

When is a "Mother's son" no longer a 'Mother's son"?

Is protocol always appropriate in every situation?

The age-old question runs on: which is better, to have loved and been rejected or never to have loved at all?

Can a human love what he now has more than what he hopes to have?

What advantage does the righteous one have over the unrighteous? Is not their end the same?

Is what a person learns by default of more value than what has deliberately learned?

Why does Almighty God grant some of the wicked longer lives than the righteous?

Who does society abhor the most, the Rush Limbaughs or the ultra Liberals?

Is it an accurate assumption that the ultra-conservative Republicans such as radio talk show host Rush Limbaugh is less compassionate and understanding of minorities than the likes of comedian Bill Maher who can always be counted on to soften a somber mood or lambast the Living God?

Why do some religious institutions demand that their clergy abstain from all sexual activity, when it is obviously being practiced by many behind closed doors?

Does an infant know when it is falling or is it merely reacting to the fright displayed by the mother seeing the baby falling?

Can persons define the righteousness of God to the extent that they can live according to His definition and be acceptable to Almighty God?

Where can an individual go to escape the rigors of life and still be counted among those who do not retreat in the day of battle?

Is a human his own worst enemy or is there one he has not met worse than he?

Are humans ever capable of giving Agape love to another independently of God?

How can a bird fly thousands of miles to a destination not previously known?

How can a salmon return to her original birthplace after having traveled thousands of miles in the vast waters of the seas?

Who or what tells a human when death is near if she has never died before?

How can one sometimes sense the presence of an enemy or a friend if no words were exchanged or other communications established?

Can a human see clearly the things she's adverse to?

Will agreeing with one's enemy make him more a friend than a foe?

Who makes the best lover, the one who has loved in the past and is experienced in the affairs of the heart or one who has never loved at all and is open to new things?

Is prosperity money driven or is money the result of prosperity?

Does God favor the giver of prosperity more than the prosperous giver?

Can one know the error of his ways without first knowing what an error is?

Can one be a politician and a Bible-believing, true worshipper of the Lord Jesus Christ at the same time?

Does a person's core values define what kind of man he is?

Is one's possessions any indicator of his moral values?

Is justice blind or only blind to those who can't afford to purchase it?

The one at the top of the heap commands the greatest respect because he or she is the one most visible.

Do you always know best or is your position based solely on your personal emotions and expectations?

Lying in wait for an enemy might mean lying in wait for your death.

The term "Lily white" is a vague attempt to glorify something or someone who is "everything but," as white is not a color but an absence of color.

Who has the greater potential as a good wife, the loose woman for her experience or the less experienced woman who knows the Lord?

Which is the better hire, the one who can't write the job description but can demonstrate his abilities, or the one who can't demonstrate his abilities, but can write the job description?

Who can know right except she first know wrong?

All things have a beginning and an ending but what happens in the middle will tell the rest of the story.

Does the end of a thing always justify the means to that end?

Who is greater, the one who built a mansion or the one who occupies it?

On what grounds are humans judged, by their thoughts or the manifestations of their thoughts by their actions?

A person's end can no one know, except the one who ends it.

Is human knowledge self-perpetuating or is there an external source that generates and regenerates our understanding of ourselves and our universe?

Is human wisdom an acquired attribute originating in a source greater than ourselves or is it a product of our environment?

Can a human love a god he doesn't understand more than a God he has never seen?

Is truth a mere conjecture based on a human hope of better things in his life and the lives of those around him or is human hope based on an unfulfilled promise of things greater than ourselves or experiences felt but not seen?

Humorous

Someone once said, "Hold on to your hat, you're about to move." Better yet, be prepared to jump.

A hole in a wall is far better than a hole in the head and a long walk home better than a night of terror and shame.

Who knows when the fat lady will sing for she too has time issues.

It is sometimes suggested that one should not "Buy a pig in the poke." Who knows what you're buying? It may be a terrorist or somebody in drag.

"A bird in the hand is better than two in the bush" is true because the two in the bush may have left or never arrived.

Never ask someone to walk a mile in your shoes. They might keep going and you'll lose your shoes.

Myth: Jack and Jill never went up a hill to get a pail of water. However, water does not run up hill. This lie never seems to fade away, but seems to live forever.

Question: Why was Humpty-Dumpty so dumb as to sit on a wall, and when he fell why they didn't call a physician instead of horses is beyond me! Where was the physician?

Those who play with dogs can expect to be licked on the lips.

Is a woman's ardor an indication of the degree of her fidelity or her fidelity an indication of the depth of her ardor?

"Don't throw the baby out with the bath water. If the "baby" is not worth keeping, why not?

"Don't let your right hand know what your left hand is doing." This is not good advice because you're dividing your body into secret compartments if you do that!

"Don't bite the hand that feeds you." Why not? Alternate between taking the food and then nipping at the hand.

'Let sleeping dogs lie." Good advice because the one sleeping may be your worst nightmare.

When told that someone needed a hand, a lady replied, "That's their red wagon." My question is: Why on earth did it have to be a "red' wagon, why not pink?

While walking toward the back of the church during a service, why do some hold up a finger as they walk? Are they saying; "Be quiet, I'm walking!"

Why in some churches does everyone turn around and look at those entering the church but refuse to send them a smile.

What's "Good for the goose" is not necessarily "Good for the gander." Suppose one likes cheese and the other corn?

Someone suggested: "You wash my back and I'll wash yours." No, no. I don't like the inference here!

Beware of the singing fat lady for she too, may have a price she can't pay.

LaVergne, TN USA
08 July 2010
188825LV00002B/2/P